Previous Books

Healing by Contacting Your Cells.
Journal Excerpts from the Ring of Fire.
What Can You Do To Help Our World?
2013 And Beyond.
2013 And Beyond Part II.
2014 World Journals.
2015 World Healing.
2015 World Healing II.
2016 World Journals.
2016 World Journals II.
Memories 2017.
Memories 2017 Part 11.

http://www.globalmeditations.com

Note: http://www.globalmeditations.com opens with the book listing giving cover photos, chapter names, etc.

2018 AUSTRALIA & JAPAN JOURNEYS

Barbara Wolf & Margaret Anderson

authorHOUSE®

AuthorHouse™
1663 Liberty Drive
Bloomington, IN 47403
www.authorhouse.com
Phone: 1 (800) 839-8640

Published by AuthorHouse 08/06/2018

ISBN: 978-1-5462-5429-4 (sc)
ISBN: 978-1-5462-5427-0 (hc)
ISBN: 978-1-5462-5428-7 (e)

Library of Congress Control Number: 2018909235

Photo taken by Margaret's cellphone. Margaret is feeding a kangaroo and Barbara is watching.

This book is dedicated to Barbara's husband Jack
and to the rest of the world.

ACKNOWLEDGEMENTS

Masami Saionji
Hideo Nakazawa
Hiroyoshi Kawagishi
Rei, Hiro's wife
Mieko Sakai
Mitsuru Ooba
Kazuyuki Namatame
Keiko Nakamichi
Fumi Johns Stewart
Masami Kichimi
Stella Edmundson
Macky Edmundson
Chief Golden Light Eagle
Grandmother SilverStar
Annelis Kessler
David J Adams
John Stafford
Davion Atkins
Alfred Hankins
Donald Pearson
Robert Ziefel
Andy Blair
Joan Lenhard
Lisa Asito

FOREWORD

We firmly believe in what we believe, and we realize you may not agree with everything we believe. Probably we would not agree with everything you agree with. But let us put aside our differences and let us be friends.

It's the world that matters. Mother Earth needs help and we are trying to give it to her. That is all that is expected.

CONTENTS

INTRODUCTION

Chapter 1. On the cover of this book are kangaroos we met just after arriving in Australia. It was fun meeting them! We stayed on what is called the Sunshine Coast and we were close to the ocean. Every moment was remarkable. We saw magnificent tall trees once used for food by the Aborigines. We saw the Glass House Mountains that are ancient volcanic plugs.

Chapter 2. Our next focus is Ayers Rock, the largest rock in the world. It has tremendous power and is esoterically connected to eleven other major places on the planet. We also tell you about the Aborigines who maintain a stronghold on Ayers Rock because it is a major power site on Mother Earth.

Chapter 3. We take a helicopter ride to see Ayers Rock, which Margaret calls Uluru because it is an Aborigine name. Then we fly to the Olgas which Margaret calls Kata Tjuta. Later, we physically visit both of them.

Chapter 4. Now our attention is on Alice Springs, another powerful Australian place where there were rivers before the land became a desert. Today, outlines of big rivers are on the desert floor and the water is beneath them. When rain comes now, often the outlines of the rivers are filled in with water. Then we go to Corroboree Rock, another important Australian place once celebrated by ancient Aborigines. We feel their ancient, powerful energy.

Chapter 5. Now we go to Japan to prepare to talk on our book, Healing By Contacting Your Cells. In Tokyo, we visit a shrine that has karma that we think needs to be removed.

Chapter 6. For us, this will be a big day because we will give our talk. We meet Japanese friends who have prepared this for us.

Chapter 7. After completing our talks, we are taken to the home of a Japanese friend who lives in the countryside among big trees and large rice fields. This friend takes us to a nearby Pacific Ocean beach where, a couple years ago, we saw a child nearly drown because of fierce winds and pounding surf. This time, to our joy, we witness mild wind and surf.

Chapter 8. On May 20, we are driven to a location close to sacred Mount Fuji where we attend a Symphony of Peace Prayers event. This celebrates the concept of The Fuji Declaration which concentrates on the creation of a Divine Spark that would unite all humanity in recognizing the value and dignity of each and every life. Thousands come across the world to attend, and we are Guests of Honor.

Chapter 9. Now we are again staying close to the Pacific Ocean with our friend who is restoring his house according to ancient times when everything exterior and interior was made from Nature. There were no plastic or artificial materials. Here, we speak to an assembled audience about our book, Healing By Contacting Your Cells, which has been translated and published in Japanese. All have copies in their hands for us to sign.

Chapter 10. This chapter has excerpts from Barbara's 1989 visit to Australia because a technique called Agnihotra was used then to take away negativity. It has been proved that Agnihotra can take away radiation negativity. We are concerned today that Japan remains affected by the 2011 nuclear accident. We think the use of Agnihotra would be helpful.

CHAPTER 1

Sunshine Coast, Australia

From Barbara:

We are ready to leave for Australia and Japan and our first attention will be the Sunshine Coast of Australia.

While we are preparing our journey, we learn that Mother Earth is experiencing shifts, and twenty-two shifts are expected this year. They will make one feel uncomfortable, a bit nervous, a bit upset. This will continue for a day, maybe two days, and then the unrest within us is gone.

Fortunately, those who know about shifts have sent out this message and we have read it.

Humanity is only a portion of what is living on this planet. Is there evidence of shifts being felt by the land? My thought is that these shifts, if felt by the land, would be felt as earth eruptions, quakes, volcanic explosions.

We learn that if Mother Earth decides to begin an extensive eruption on her surface, she will begin this eruption in the Pacific Ocean in the area we call Hawaii. Molten lava will come from the center of Mother Earth to her surface. If Hawaii is not hit first, then attention should be focused on Japan being hit first.

Just as we are ready to begin our journey, we learn that on May 3, Hawaii encountered a very big eruption. Should we cancel our journey which begins on May 5? Our suitcases are ready to go. What should we do? Go or not go?

Faith, we realize. We need faith that we are behaving properly. We will go. First we will go to the Sunshine Coast in Australia and then we will go to Japan to speak two times.

May 5:

We take a short flight from Rochester to Chicago where a Qantas flight flies us across the continent to Los Angeles. This is the first time we have taken a Qantas flight and we are impressed. Our flight is full and two middle-aged stewards and some female stewardesses accommodate us, all smiling. They give out beautiful, well-designed menus that make our mouths water as we read.

When we reach the West Coast near the location of Los Angeles, the sun has left us and it is dark. I look down at lights extending for miles along the water line, and I realize a huge population lives here. Big, lighted highways stretch here and there. Lighted buildings are everywhere. Yes, there are many who live here.

Interesting, between Margaret and me sits a male, probably in his twenties, who is returning to his home in Los Angeles. He says he loves the place and he is happy to come home again. He comes home as often as possible.

We change planes in Los Angeles and this next plane, headed to Brisbane, Australia, is jammed with people going home. I cannot sleep and so most of the night I watch the screen in front of me showing the location of the plane -- where it is going, the names of the places we will be passing, etc. When we reach the Equator, the screen says our watches need to move forward.

The screen also shows Brisbane's location to Tokyo which is where we will go after leaving Australia. Yes, the screen in front of me is fun to watch because it shows our locations for the next eighteen days.

Now Margaret will tell us about the beginning of her trip.

From Margaret:

Packing for this trip to Australia and Japan is very complex because I need to take many folders and files in my carry-on bag. When we are ready, Joan the taxi driver arrives and we are soon at the Rochester Airport where we are given boarding passes for Chicago, Los Angeles, and Brisbane, Australia.

In Chicago, our gate for Los Angeles is far across the airport from where we land. To transfer for our next flight, we must go through a new section of the airport. This does not include the towering dinosaur skeleton we are accustomed to seeing and we are sad. At our proper departure gate, we settle in for a two-hour wait.

When it is time to board, our seatmate is a young man from Los Angeles and Chicago who is delightful and enthusiastic when he speaks. As we move along, I think of the continent below us and I send out thoughts of calm across the country which I feel is unsettled. When we reach the West Coast, I place my mind on the dolphins and whales traveling up the coast.

On arrival at the Los Angeles Airport, we must reach a far gate where large Qantas airplanes are parked. Our Qantas plane to Brisbane is a new one and we are given seats in row 54. The stewards and stewardesses are extremely kind and attentive, and they serve a delicious dinner before most everyone begins to sleep. I rest and then explore the screen in front of me showing me a series of engineering miracles about present-day technology based on past discoveries. I watch films ranging from the design of the earliest wooden roller coaster to the newest world radio telescope, and life on the space station.

My mind is uplifted by the dedication of past and present scientists and engineers bettering life on the planet. I love so much the English astronaut saying that everyone works for the good of the mission and everyone shares knowledge and experience for the betterment of the whole. These words uplift me because I know humans need to live on this planet by cooperating and sharing.

After long hours of flying toward Brisbane, our plane crosses the Equator and International Dateline. Here I connect to the whole Pacific and I send deep into the ocean a beam of radiant crystalline Light full of healing, Love, peace, and appreciation. I know the Light spreads deep into the ocean.

When we approach the continent of Australia, I acknowledge the Aborigines who so carefully held the land. I address their ancestors and guardians of the land. I telepathically send out a message that we are coming to Australia to honor and to give gratitude for their stewardship of the land and its inhabitants – human, animals, birds, reptiles, plants and all life forms.

It is a privilege to be here.

From Barbara:

May 7:

When night becomes day, May 7, the pilot is ready to land in Brisbane and he brings the plane down smoothly. As he moves us to the terminal, I am surprised at the size of this airport. It is huge. Los Angeles and Chicago are big, but I do not expect Brisbane to be in that category.

When we exit the plane, I have in my hands a customs form warning me that if I do not answer its questions correctly, I will be caught and punished. I am worried about my energy bars and I show them. WHEW. They pass.

I go with many passengers here and there, up elevators, down escalators, and finally we are at doors opening to the outside. Now we have a new concern. Where is Macky, son of Stella, Margaret's sister, who will pick us up and take us to the home of his mother? Many people are waiting for their rides and we do not see him.

Well, we have to be patient. Maybe he is late for some reason. In less than fifteen minutes he joins us and tells us to follow him to his car. There are many, many cars and he says it has taken him forty minutes to find a place to park.

When we reach his bright red car, I open the door and of course I have forgotten he drives on the wrong side of the road, as I call driving British style rather than American style. Without comment, he opens the back door and puts me in.

Now he drives slowly, passing many parked cars until we reach a road that connects us to a main road taking us north to his mother's home. I expect this road to be busy and I am amazed at how few cars are using this road. However, Macky has told us today is a holiday, which, to me, indicates many are not driving today.

As we go along smoothly, I notice we are passing no houses. Only big, beautiful forests. Miles and miles of green forests. No humans, I am thinking, have planted them. They have come up on their own.

I am also thinking I do not feel the energy of the Aborigines who once lived in this forested area and I do not think they are living here now. That was the past, before the country became occupied by foreigners. In any case, I enjoy looking out the window at magnificent trees.

Finally we reach population and there is strong evidence that trees living alone are now living with houses. We pass a farming area where kangaroos are munching on the land.

When we reach Stella's house, it is wonderful meeting her again!

From Margaret:

Before 6:00 a.m. we land in Brisbane and pass through customs easily. Soon we are with my sister Stella's son, Macky Edmundson, and he is driving us to her house on the Sunshine Coast of Queensland. Traffic is light because it is a holiday, Labor Day. I watch from the window magnificent forests growing. There are no houses.

It is wonderful to be with Stella again in her home. From the U.S.A., I often talk with her by phone, but there is nothing more wonderful than being with my sister in person.

She is a visionary artist and her home is filled with magnificent artwork displayed on the walls. Barbara and I admire her framed hooked rugs that show exquisite scenes of animals and birds of Australia and ancient life and pageantry of India. Her home is alive with Light and Love of creativity.

We also like her two cats who are hiding under the bed waiting to be convinced that they will be okay if they come out to be petted.

Stella soon has food on the table for us and we sit and eat and happily talk. Also, we begin making plans. First, we want to see the waters of the Pacific.

Is this water choppy and upset or is this water calm? What is its attitude?

From Barbara:

After our meal, Macky drives us to the ocean which is close to Stella's house, but we have not seen it because of magnificent tall trees blocking the ocean view from the road.

As he parks the car at the beginning of a dirt pathway, we can hear the mighty big roar of the ocean but we cannot see it. A powerful wind nearly takes our heads off as we get out of the car to walk toward the ocean we cannot see.

Now we reach a viewing platform overlooking a beach with the water beyond. But, we realize the wind is so powerful, we cannot go farther. We stand and watch the mighty waves and we are sad we cannot go to them. Tomorrow will be a better day to visit, we decide, and we turn and follow the dirt pathway to the road and the car.

From Margaret:

After a delicious breakfast, Macky takes us to the ocean, which is quite nearby. I have sacred healing symbols with me for the ocean, but the wind is too strong and the ocean is too rough for me to draw the healing Symbols.* I need to wait another day.

*See Glossary: Vortex Symbols.

Now Macky takes us to the top of a forested hill where we can see the distant Glass House Mountains,* volcanic plugs now exposed by millions of years of wind, rain and soil erosion. In one direction we can see the Glass House Mountains, and in the other direction we can see the ocean. What magic! There is amazing power here!

*See Glossary: Glass House Mountains.

Now we go to the Eric Joseph Foote Nature Reserve in Buderim, a park of ancient trees and flowers. I see a forest of tall magnificent trees and I am drawn to looking up at their impressive canopy. I also marvel at the root system that holds these sacred trees in place.

Signs tell us of the early use of these trees by the Aborigines who were keepers of this land. Not many are not here in the present but the Aborigine Spirits, ancestors and guardians are here in feeling and presence. We cherish our walk in the complexity of the nature world -- the trees, soil, ocean and forest -- the vast complexity of Australia.

From Barbara:

When Macky takes us to Eric Joseph Foote Park, we walk along a pathway to view magnificent tall trees that have been here many many years. I have a strong feeling of the energy of the Aborigines. They knew these trees. They were comfortable with this place. We walk along a pathway and stop to read signs explaining about specific trees. The first tree has a sign saying it was used as food by Aborigines and birds that had a name I do not know. Then we walk to another tree with a sign explaining about Aborigines and these trees.

Yes, this is interesting. I feel I am in the homeland of the Aborigines. Their energy is quite different from the present-day Australian owners.

From Margaret:

On our return to Stella's home, we are gifted by seeing kangaroo families in an open field. Also, today we have heard parrots and cockatoos and we have seen the mountains and the ocean. I feel deeply blessed.

May 8:

From Barbara:

When we were in Australia a few years ago, we went to the zoo to see the kangaroos and it was a wonderful experience. My thought is that the kangaroos have been living on this continent a very, very long time. They represent ancient animals still on this planet, which means they represent ancient Earth still managing at this present day. Even though the Earth is now probably more upset than earlier, they still seem to manage. They knew the Aborigines and the Aborigines knew them. I connect Australia with both.

This morning, Stella drives us to the zoo to see the kangaroos. As she is driving, I watch the multitude of tall green trees we are passing. I know they like water. As for myself, I realize the weather today is being kind to us. It is not raining and not too cold or too hot.

When we arrive at the zoo, Stella drops us at the entrance and she drives the car away to park it. Although we see many parked cars, we do not see any people because they are already inside the zoo. When she returns to us, we buy food to feed the kangaroos and then we begin our walk to them. First, we pass enclosures for huge turtles that I remember from an earlier visit.

Now we are following signs saying we are walking in the right direction to reach the kangaroos. And yes, soon we are among them. But, I am surprised they are lying on the ground, sprawled all over the place. They do not seem interested in eating. Some people are among them offering food, but their attempts fail.

However, we now see at the edge of a pathway a mother wallaby smaller than a kangaroo eating food from the hand of a visitor. What is so remarkable is that a tiny, tiny baby is sticking his head out of his mother's pouch as she is eating. What fun to watch this!

Now we walk a bit further to reach about ten disinterested kangaroos sprawled on the ground. We are thinking, will they allow us to be photographed with them? Maybe such a photograph would be good for the cover of our book.

A man with a camera is standing nearby. Will he take our photograph with the kangaroos? Yes. With Margaret's cellphone.

When that is accomplished, we have thoughts of checking on what is happening just ahead of us. There is an outdoor stadium where people are beginning to gather for a crocodile performance. We have never seen a crocodile performance, and so we gather with them to sit on chairs in the stadium.

However, the performance does not begin with crocodiles. Instead, colorful birds are released to fly across the stadium from one end to the other. Some swoop close to us, and I note they are not afraid.

I know these birds are living in captivity at the zoo, but I am curious they seem controlled and will not fly away. Then I see zoo members sitting in the audience with food in their hands. The birds are flying from one food source to another. They are used to doing this. When the food is over and their flying performance is over, they are used to returning to their zoo home.

When it is time for the crocodile performance, we watch as a huge dark body of a crocodile swims underwater into the stadium. He moves slowly, very slowly, as we watch. Above him, on the stadium ground surface, are zoo employees dangling dead birds from their hands. I note they are very careful about protecting themselves. And yes! They need to be careful. We watch as this huge crocodile suddenly launches his head out of the water to catch a dangling dead bird. His open mouth comes CLOSE to the hands of the park employee holding the dead bird.

When the entertainment is over, suddenly it begins to rain hard and we take shelter to wait for it to stop. Well, the rain seems to have no intention of quitting. We wait patiently and when it does stop, we climb aboard a free shuttle tram which shelters passengers from any chance of more rain. One of its destinations is the entrance to the zoo, and here we leave the tram and Stella drives us to her home.

Later in the afternoon, we return to the beach which we tried to see yesterday when the wind and waves were TOO POWERFUL. Today, the water is calm. The beach is inviting.

From Margaret

May 8:

As Barbara has just told you, this morning Stella drives us to the Australia Zoo to see the kangaroos. Here, we buy three packages of kangaroo food of corn and grains. To reach them, we pass two large turtles eating their breakfast of dark leaves.

Then we walk to Roo Heaven, the area devoted to wallabies and kangaroos, and we are remembering the last time we were here. They were completely tame and enjoyed eating from the outstretched hands of visitors. But, to our surprise today, the feeding desire is over, and they are sprawled on their sides to enjoy the moist grass and the attention of the people.

I try to feed a small wallaby and it hops away because of no interest in eating. Then we walk to a large group of kangaroos to have our picture taken with them. Perhaps it will be the cover of our book.

When we leave the kangaroos, we go to a large stadium to sit on chairs to watch the zoo staff entertain with birds and a crocodile. I enjoy watching the birds in their beautiful flight.

After the entertainment, it begins to rain in torrents and we decide to take the covered tram that goes around the park. This, we discover, is a bonus because we can see the vastness of the park. The rain has made everything even more beautiful.

After returning to Stella's home and at dusk we go to Mudjimba Beach that we had abandoned the day before because of rough weather. But today the ocean is calm and the beach is calm. And now that the water is calm, the beautiful white beach has expanded greatly. However, I notice rain clouds forming and we need to be vigilant.

I go to the water to address the ocean, the whales, dolphins and all life forms. I wish to honor the ocean with a gift of Love and Healing in the form of Sacred Symbols that I will draw on the hard sand.

I begin drawing these twenty-two Symbols at the water's edge and when I am finished, the rain comes. This rain actually helps give the gift to the ocean.

AUM.

CHAPTER 2

First Days in Australia

From Barbara:

May 9:

This morning, Margaret and I will take transport to Brisbane Airport where we will stay at a nearby hotel for the night in order to be ready for a very early morning flight to Sydney and then to Ayers Rock. Why are we going to Ayers Rock, the largest rock in the world? It has tremendous power and is esoterically connected to eleven major places on the planet that are energized by galactic energies.

For a great number of years, the Aborigines had maintained a strong hold on this place because it is a major power site on Mother Earth. Now, because of non-Aborigines flocking to Ayers Rock, the Aborigines have shifted the power to the Olga Mountains, situated quite close to Ayers Rock. In a couple days, we will ride a helicopter specifically to see these two locations and put our energies on them.

This morning, a few minutes before 10 a.m., a limousine arrives and a pleasant driver puts our bags into the vehicle and we are on our way to Brisbane Airport.

As we move along, the driver talks to us in such a friendly manner, the conversation holds throughout the one-hour and fifteen minute journey. We quickly learn that he was a soldier in the Vietnam War, and he has lived all over the place during his lifetime. He tells us his mother began a job on a tour boat when she was fifteen and she eventually had six children.

From Margaret:

In the pre-dawn morning, I wake thinking about the etheric reality of the Sacred Glass House Mountains I saw yesterday. I now receive the understanding that they exist in higher dimensions and their energy reflects on the third dimensional mountains below. As above, so below. I relish the comprehension of this transfer of power.

But now I must change my thoughts to Brisbane because we will stay overnight in order to fly very early the following day to Sydney and Ayers Rock (Uluru).

In the morning, a limousine shuttle driver takes us to Brisbane. And while he is driving, he says he drives a school bus for children and he transports pilots for Qantas. At the age of thirteen, he tells us, his father became a cabin boy who later became a sea captain. His mother was a sea stewardess at fifteen. Both were from London. Our driver knew all the stories about Captain Cook running aground and patching up his boat to sail again. These were delightful stories to hear. Also, he tells us there is a resident family of kangaroos on his property. He says kangaroos come visiting because his family has two cats and no dogs. I love hearing these wonderful stories.

From Barbara:

When we arrive at the ibis Brisbane Airport Hotel, I see it is a very large, modern hotel close to the Brisbane Airport. The driver takes our bags to the front desk and leaves as we are asking the woman at the front desk if we have arrived too early for a room to be available. She, in a friendly manner, says the normal time to enter a room is 2 p.m. We are horrified! It is 11 a.m. But, she says, never mind. A room is ready and we can have it now. She will help us go to our room and she takes my suitcase and rolls it to a nearby elevator. Then she shows us how to place our room card on a button inside the elevator so the elevator will respond. Oh dear! There is always so much to learn.

Our room 617 at the top of the hotel overlooks a huge expanse of the city of Brisbane. Most important is that our room overlooks the close-by airport building where we will go tomorrow to catch a flight to Sydney. From Sydney, we will catch another flight to Ayres Rock. Our plane tomorrow will leave at 7 a.m. and we are pleased this hotel is so close to our departure.

Now it is time to think about eating, and we return to the first floor to have lunch at an eating area close to the front desk. Only one person is eating. Where is everyone? Never mind. We are given a menu with many selections and after examining them, we decide to eat a child's selection of fish and chips, orange juice and ice cream. Perfect!

Our overnight stay at the ibis Brisbane Airport Hotel is comfortable and we sleep well. And yes, a huge advantage has been to be so close to our departure area at an early hour. It is daylight when we walk a couple minutes to check in for our flight. Actually, I have been surprised at the daylight. It has been so cold at home, my thoughts are still on winter and dark mornings.

From Margaret:

May 10:

During the night, I begin thinking about the wildlife ambassadors of Australia superimposed on the ancient lands of the Aborigines. These are the sweet birds in the rain forests, the kangaroos, the wallabies, and the koala bears.

Perhaps I should inscribe in the air my gift of the sacred healing Symbols and Vortexes to the Aborigines rather than draw them on the land. The Aborigines are from other star systems and so they will understand the Symbols.

I also think of Stella giving us Glass House Mountains crystals. She said they never belonged to her. I feel the powerful draw of the Glass House Mountains as well as other sacred mountains, sacred waters, sacred trees, sacred birds, sacred sea creatures, sacred land creatures.

AUM.

Toward morning, I realize I must switch off my mind probing and switch to my heart. This will open the door to the Aborigine frequency and the understanding of today's work of Ayers Rock which I call Uluru.

In the early morning at Brisbane, we check out of the hotel and walk a couple minutes to the airline terminal where we easily go through Security. Then we go to gate 39 where we depart a 7:00 a.m.

Our flight is one hour and fifteen minutes to Sydney and when we land, we transfer to the gate where a large modern plane will fly us to Ayers Rock. This is a three and one-half hour flight.

When we leave Sydney, at first the landscape is green and wooded with mist over valleys between the mountains. Then there is a long stretch with complete cloud cover. When the clouds disappear, the land below is sparse, like a desert. But suddenly I see white beneath me that seems to be salt framing great bodies of water. Suddenly, in the sky above the water, I see clouds appearing in the form of racing dolphins and whales rushing to Uluru (Ayers Rock). Magical! This scene continues a long time.

From Barbara:

When we are flying and I perceive we are coming close to Ayers Rock, the pilot announces that those sitting on the left side of the plane will be able to see Ayers Rock.

We look down and I see red rock! The pilot begins inching along, slowing the plane to a point where it does not feel like we are hardly moving. I know we are flying directly over Ayers Rock. We are so close to its massive top, I can see all the cracks and crevices at the top of this red phenomenon. Then the pilot picks up speed and we are quickly at the airport.

Here, another plane has just landed and probably over one hundred people are waiting for bags. Well, patience is needed, and we note that everyone seems patient.

When we pick up our bags, we board a free bus to take us to our hotel -- the Outback Pioneer. As the driver goes along, we look out the windows and sure enough, far away, we see Ayers Rock. Wonderful! It is red and beautiful. Very beautiful!

Now that we have arrived in the vicinity of Ayers Rock, I begin hearing people using the word Uluru rather than Ayers Rock. I assume this is an Aborigine name, but I will use Ayers Rock and Margaret will use Uluru.

From Margaret:

I too see Uluru from the plane. ULURU!! There it is!! In a flash -- visible and invisible. I see this sacred mountain but only for a few seconds and then my eyes are closed. My hands, inner Light, become hot, full of healing energy from this sacred place. I mentally name people needing healing and I hold this healing focus, thinking that everyone will be touched by Uluru's healing power.

In my mind, I see a visionary tunnel, a shaft going into the mountain with spiritual treasures to be discovered. I want to touch the mountain but I am told that in order to hold the healing power, I cannot use my hands to touch. I must touch with my heart and not with my hands. I feel this is a gift from the Aborigines.

When we land at Ayers Rock, we catch a bus to the Outback Pioneer Hotel where we are given Room 104 on the ground floor. We look out our window at green trees beside the hotel.

Now we begin to make plans. We want to take Hop On Hop Off buses to Uluru and Kata Tjuta (The Olgas).* Donald Pearson at the Information Desk helps us. He understands when Barbara says the Aborigines are present today to help the Earth at this crucial time.

*See Glossary: Map of Uluru and Kata Tjuta.

In the evening, we order pizza to be cooked for us at a kitchen connected to the hotel. We eat this delicious pizza in our room before calling it quits for today.

From Barbara:

We sign up for a next day morning bus ride journey around Ayers Rock and in the afternoon we will take a helicopter ride to Ayers

Rock as well as to the Olgas. They are connected to each other even though they are thirty miles apart. From Ayers Rock, land submerges and stays underground before rising to become the Olgas.

The Aborigines have always regarded Ayers Rock as a very sacred place.

Great ceremonies were performed here. But, when foreigners took over the land, the Aborigines turned their attention more to the Olgas.

CHAPTER 3

Ayers Rock (Uluru), The Olgas (Kata Tjuta)

F rom Margaret:

May 11:

1:10 a.m. in meditation, as a gift of healing, I esoterically place the Vortex Ring of sacred Symbols on Uluru, Mother Earth's Sacred Mountain.

I speak to the Aborigines, ancestors of the land, acknowledging their care and love.

I place my hands in room water to draw the Symbols and mentally speak the name of each Symbol, each Vortex, for power and healing.

I send out the energy of the water blessed by the Vortexes to the land.

Pure water -- blessed water, gift to Uluru, to the Aborigines present, future and past -- caretakers of the land and all life forms.

The water energy kisses the land.

AUM.

A gift of Love to Uluru.

At 8:40 a.m. Barbara and I are on a Hop On Hop Off shuttle bus to take us to Uluru. We ask the young male driver which side to sit on for the best view of Uluru, and he points to the left.

We are soon speedily on our way to this massive sandstone rock formation rising up above the desert. On the plane yesterday, I felt strongly the presence of Uluru but I saw its physical form only a few seconds before my eyes were closed in meditation.

Today, when I am looking for the huge rock formation sacred to the Aborigines, at first I see only individual trees and silver grasses glistening in the sun. Then, YES, Uluru appears! Uluru looms above the horizon.

There it is!

It is a dream of a lifetime to physically view the magnificent rock structure, massive and complex. I examine the powerful ridges, the layers of rock pointed upward, etc.

As the bus speeds along, I photograph and the camera jumps into action -- click, click, video, black and white, color, multiple pictures. I cannot control the camera but I can hold on and hope for a few good shots.

When we are closer to Uluru, I put my camera away and use my heart and eyes to film. I want my heart to record the experience. The camera gets in the way. The recording is eternal -- internal.

The Hop On Hop Off bus circles Uluru moving from west to north to east to south so we can see the different sides from all different angles. Different faces of Uluru. Different aspects.

When I see climbers ascending this sacred rock, I do not look at them.

Now I receive a channeling:

The place is sacred. Would people climb Chartres Cathedral sacred to the world Christians? Why climb Uluru, sacred to the Aborigines? Nature needs to be honored in its own way. Not by walking on it but by cherishing it, holding it up like a sacred chalice, a sacred new born baby, a Sacred Mountain to Love with the heart and soul. Not by touching with feet.

Climbing this sacred rock mountain is not an exercise event. Being in its presence is a sacred understanding that opens the door to other outer and inner worlds.

Be a Caretaker as instructed by the Aborigines in the welcoming film seen upon arrival at the airport.

I am happy the sacred significance of Uluru will be respected on October 26, 2019 when the climb will be closed permanently.

October 26 is the anniversary date of when the Governor General of Australia in ceremony handed back the title deeds to the Uluru-Kata Tjuta National Park to the Traditional Owners of the land, the (Aborigine) Anangu People. This happened on October 26, 1985.*

*See Glossary: Closing the Uluru climb.

Today, as we are circling Uluru in our shuttle bus, I am delighted to be here.

This afternoon we will take a helicopter ride to Uluru and Kata Tjuta (The Olgas). But I must admit that earlier in April, when thinking about booking a helicopter, I worried about the appropriateness of flying near such a sacred site. Then the ancient Aborigines came in and said they will join us. They will be with us. And so I never thought about it again.

From Barbara:

This morning, at 8:40 a.m., when Margaret and I wait outside the hotel for a van to take us to Ayers Rock, we note that drivers are coming to and going from this hotel. There is free transportation to the airport and trips to other places. When our van arrives, about six people board with us to circle Ayers Rock. I am excited to be in the van because I have waited patiently for this visit. I think it has been nearly thirty years since I was last here.

The van driver who picks us up goes speedily as I watch out the window. I note there are a number of trees growing in the area. When I was last here, there were few trees. I also note the lack of flowers. Earlier, there were many. The ranger who took me earlier was continually remarking at the number of wild flowers he had not seen for many years. Much rain had brought them. Well, I see no flowers now but I see many more trees than earlier. Have they been deliberately planted?

As we come closer and closer to Ayers Rock, I see people in one long line climbing to the top. Hundreds, I think. Some are at the very top.

I can understand why the Aborigines have moved their sacred spot to the Olgas.

More from Barbara:

This afternoon we take a helicopter ride to see Ayers Rock and the Olgas from the air. We will be picked up at the front of the hotel and, as we wait for a car to pick us up, we sit in the sunshine because it is very cold today.

Our ride is a bit late and I worry the helicopter will leave without us, but it is waiting for us. Interesting, the car goes directly to the waiting helicopter and within moments we are aboard. This is the first time I have flown in a helicopter, and it would be easy to be nervous, but I refuse to think about nervousness. I sit back and relax. This will be a wonderful trip!

Big, thick protective earphones are given to me and I am firmly strapped in with crisscross seat belts. Then the pilot begins moving us upward, and this is done in a gentle way. No jerking back and forth and side by side as I would expect. Immediately, he moves us toward Ayers Rock which is quite close to us. I look down at this big, red structure standing alone by itself, and I have a feeling it is lonesome. There are no other structures to keep it company.

I note that the land has maturing green trees, and this is land I remember earlier as being without much vegetation, including few trees. In fact, I do not remember any trees. From the air, I can see the trees having been deliberately planted.

As for Ayers Rock, the pilot makes sharp turns around and around the rock so we have an opportunity to see it well. When he decides we have seen enough, he heads us to the Olgas which I see is composed of thirty big ridges of sandstone. I know the Olgas are connected to

Barbara Wolf & Margaret Anderson

Ayers Rock. They are considered to be million of years old and over the years, they have lost their height.

The pilot spends only a short time here and then he returns us to a helicopter pad.

Well, the trip was wonderful! I take off my huge earphones, climb out of the helicopter and wave goodbye to the pilot.

From Margaret about the helicopter ride:

3:30 p.m., Professional Helicopter Services pick us up to go to their trailer office to see a movie on the safety of riding a helicopter. This is a first for both Barbara and myself.

At the helicopter pad, we have our pictures taken before we board. There are five in our group. I sit at the window in the back and feel very comfortable strapped in wearing huge earphones with speakers and a microphone. I am so excited, I cannot say a word. My speaking facility is turned off. My ears work and my eyes work but I am unable to speak.

However, I am calm, relaxed and enjoying every moment.

I try to use my camera but after a moment I put it down to focus on the ride.

I enjoy the excitement of approaching Uluru, then circling it. I study carefully the ground surrounding it because of interesting patterns of mounds, rocks, circles, and some snake-like forms.

I love gliding and hovering in view of the sacred structure of Uluru with its ridges clearly visible in the late afternoon sun. We fly around Uluru, never over it, and I feel this is gentle respect.

26

Then the helicopter moves us to Kata Tjuta (the Olgas), and the mounds/mountains are delightful in their individuality. They are connected beneath the surface to Uluru and they hold the power of both places. In the presence of Kata Tjuta, I have the feeling of the Divine Feminine.

Later in the day, after the journey is over, I review this sacred day and I receive a channeling:

The power here is Light. Powerful Sun Disc -- broad expanse of land holding the power of the Earth Mother.

Mother Earth receives power from the centering of her center, from the strength of the rock layers and the layers of prayers and ceremony. Listen to the rocks and stones. They hold the history and the creativity of the land and the people who care for the land. Prayer Gardens.

Walk mindfully in this Prayer Garden. Do not step on the plants. Do not climb or walk in fragile areas. Keep to the path. Walk tenderly. Tend carefully all plants, animals, humans of all ages from the littlest to the largest. From the youngest to the oldest.

The land is millions and millions of years old. Respect that. Humans are just a dot in time. Open your heart and head to take that in. Care for the land and one another. Link up to your Brothers and Sisters of Beyond. Open all senses to take this in. Open your heart, mind and soul to take in the vast picture. Uluru has the key.

Message from other worlds. Guardians of the land.

From Barbara:

May 12:

Today is May 12 and after a good night's sleep, which is only interrupted a short time because our room is too cold and we do not know now how to use the heater. Margaret goes for help and very quickly an assistant comes to show us how to turn on the heater. When it starts, we are thrilled to feel the warmth!

We get up early this morning to take a Hop On Hop Off bus to the Olgas to see the sunrise which many like to see. Fortunately, there is no rain, but, oh dear, it is very cold.

We are surprised to see so many people in front of the hotel waiting for buses to take them here and there. Our bus comes, and the driver, with papers in his hands, sees our names on them and tells us to get in. We sit directly behind him.

He is a young man, probably in his mid-twenties, and he is a warm, friendly person. We are driven expertly away from the hotel and he picks up speed once we reach the road.

From the window, we can see Ayers Rock in the distance, but it is dark this early morning and we can barely see the place. There are no lights to point out this famous red rock. Now the driver picks up speed and we race along about one hundred kilometers per hour. I hope animals do not wander in the dark such as deer in my country.

The road is straight and fast and we reach the Olgas before 7 a.m. Now it is somewhat light outside so we can see where our driver wants us to walk to view the sunrise. Well, Margaret and I prefer to see the sunrise from the bus. Others leave, but after a few minutes, some return because of the cold.

When the sun has risen, all return to the bus.

What is so exciting to me is that the energy of the Olgas is wonderful. I can feel that the Aborigines are happy. They have had to remove their emphasis on Ayers Rock, but they have the Olgas. I can feel esoteric humming, esoteric activity. I am happy the non-Aborigines are respecting the wishes of the Aborigines that the Olgas need to be protected.

From Margaret:

May 12:

It is 2:00 a.m. and it is too cold to sleep. I begin walking to the main office in another building to find assistance. When I walk outside in the night, I look up and see the vast starry night spread above me – the Milky Way. A Gift!

I find a manager and he fixes our room healing system.

At 4:00 a.m. we are up and ready to catch the 5:45 a.m. Hop On Hop Off shuttle to see the Kata Tjuta sunrise. I feel and see the stars kissing Uluru, the land, and Kata Tjuta. All are Sacred.

The early morning is cold as we drive in the dark. Now we see Uluru's silhouette in the predawn light. And then we drive further to Kata Tjuta to see ancient rock formations of thirty-six domes. Among them are delicate, heart-shaped trees.

The sun appears and presses down on the crest of the rounded domes. It is 7:15 a.m., the time of dawn, the moment of the arrival of the crystalline gold Light of Love, the sun. Around it, I see a crystalline circle of Light, Love, and Healing at the horizon. The sun is dancing, spinning, spreading yellow radiance of golden Light.

I think on the extraordinary transfer of power at dawn. The time of growth, the time of healing for all the world, for all the galaxies, expanding the golden radiance of Light.

Inside the bus, I hold the Vortex Symbols for the sunrise, the light of the dawn that is visible over Kata Tjuta. The Vortexes add their energy to the dawn as I face the sun. I draw on my writing pad the silhouette of Kata Tjuta and the sun as I witness this powerful event.

Outside the bus, there are strong winds and it is very cold. Inside I am warm and I feel blessed to be here.

A message comes through from the Aborigine Guardians:

You must embrace the world to embrace us, your friends.

Tears come to my eye as the Aborigine Guardians continue to speak.

The trees, the land, are alive with loving, creative energy. These are the batteries of Mother Earth. Galactic energy transfuser -- transformer. The strength of the Aborigine presence is here. Welcome. Come in silence and in joy. This is the heartland of Australia -- Mother Earth's heartland -- close to the surface. Prayers settle on this place like spiritual lace of love and caring for the planet. All separation falls away in the unity of Spirit.

I feel the closeness here of Love frequency at Kata Tjuta. I feel the heart connect, the coding, the lock coding that opens the heart connection to Kata Tjuta. It is linked eternally, open and direct, based on Universal Galactic Love. It is expansive, vibrant, true to the land, to Mother Earth. It is held by the Aborigines and those who love Mother Earth's world and life forms and her place in the Galaxy.

Love. Love. Love. Softness. Gentleness. I feel the wind. I feel the cold. I feel the softness of the ancient hard rock. Messages have been exchanged. Songs are for singing. Lightness of Spirit rises with the sun. The trees dance. The grasses sway and glisten.

AUM.

When Barbara and I return to our hotel, I worry that I had not sufficiently used the Vortexes when I was at Kata Tjuta. Then I was told the mountains received the Vortex frequencies radiantly in the Light of Galactic energies.

Later in the afternoon when I am walking to a tourist shop close to our hotel to buy postcards, I meet Alfred Hankins, a van attendant who is Aborigine. While talking with him, I thank him for the special care of the land for centuries given by the Aborigines and for care of the people who came to this land. I tell him I came all this way to say thank you. Tears come to my eyes.

Afterwards, I meet Davion Atkins from Los Angeles who tells me he was first in training with the Voyages Indigenous Tourism Australia that operate the Ayers Rock Resort.* After training, he was hired as staff and he loves his work.

*See Glossary: Tourism businesses – Voyages; Voyages Indigenous Tourism Australia:

Davion Atkins tells me about the Training Program for Indigenous People where young people come from the cities to learn a work ethic and to learn the way of the land and culture. They can train in the hotel program. Also, they can train in international training programs. I immediately think of the young Taiwan woman I met earlier on the plane coming here. She will train six months to be a guide.

In conclusion, I want to remember and thank Davion Atkins, Donald Pearson, and Alfred Hankins, who shared their wisdom, kindness and enthusiasm with us.

CHAPTER 4

Alice Springs and Corroboree Rock

From Barbara:

May 13:

Alice Springs is our next destination and this morning we are outside the Outback Pioneer Hotel waiting for a shuttle bus to take us to the Ayers Rock Airport. But it is too cold to wait outside and so we wait inside the hotel near the front desk.

Here, we begin a conversation with a woman who is also waiting for the bus. She tells us she on vacation for a couple days, and she is an engineer, a supervisor of construction for roads. I ask her why I see red on the land when I look down from airplanes, and she explains carefully about rust coming from iron in rocks.

We begin talking about other matters as we wait and wait for the bus to take us to the airport. Where is it? It is too early in the morning for traffic jams. Where is the driver? Finally a woman from the hotel front desk investigates why we are still here. She phones, listens, and her answer to us is that the driver will come but we will have to wait. And so we wait. What more can we do?

It is at least another half hour before he arrives, and we note he is elderly and huffing and puffing. Later, one of the bus riders tells us she worried about this man. Worried about his heart.

He drives us quickly and the first thing we see is Ayers Rock in the distance. Goodbye, Ayers Rock, we hope some day to see you again.

When we finally arrive at the airport, we enter the terminal building along with twenty other people to stand in line to receive our boarding passes. Our plane is ready for us and when I find my seat, it is at a window. Good! Soon, the pilot is moving the plane slowly down a tarmac, and when it is time to take off, we take off like a shot!

Now I am looking at Australia beneath me, and again, I am amazed at the structure of this continent. It is hard to describe. One does not see towns and houses but instead, we see curious land formations. We see mountain structures as well as low, rugged land, and in another place we see white land that was once water. My thought is that this is white salt that has dried. Actually, in one place I see white water. I have been told that in the old days, the land had surface water and today it is still underground. Every three or four years, if it rains enough, water will come to the surface. Yes, I understand because, from the plane, I see land shaped like a river without water. I know the shape of this land was formed here at a time when there was water here.

Our plane is headed toward Alice Springs, and, because of its name, I expect this place has something to do with water. Interesting, when our plane lands, RAIN COMES, but only for a few moments.

As for the wording of Alice Springs, does that mean there is a water spring named after a woman? What woman?

Well, I never have figured out exactly who is the woman, but I do learn that there is water under the land that shows itself if there is enough rain. When we arrive at the airport and use a bus to reach our hotel, I look for land formations made from earlier rivers, and I do see evidence.

I am told that this place called Alice Springs is the headquarters for spreading telegraph wires across Australia to connect those living here. The name Alice comes from the wife of a supervisor, but which wife of which supervisor is in doubt and I do not investigate further.

Of interest to me is that camels were imported to take telegraph building equipment across the arid land. Today, tourists can see camels.

When our plane lands at Alice Springs, a kind airport assistant of Aborigine origin offers to help us take our baggage to a waiting bus that will take us to our hotel. We seat ourselves behind the driver who turns out to be a delightful person. He says our hotel is the last hotel he will reach, and then he will begin picking up passengers whose destination is the airport. Would we mind, he asks, if he drops off first the other bus passengers, and at the same time, he picks up passengers destined for the airport?

We do not mind, we tell him, and he begins the journey of hotel drop off-pick up from one hotel to another. About five hotels.

We, of course, are happy because we are getting a delightful sightseeing tour! The driver apologizes and apologizes and we tell him over and over we are having a wonderful sightseeing tour. To reach the various hotels, he takes us over most of Alice Springs.

Our hotel is the Double Tree Hotel by Hilton and it is outside Alice Springs. When we reach it, we are amazed it is such a beautiful hotel. As for why the word Hilton is tagged to our hotel, we do not know the answer.

We do learn, however, that today is a holiday – Mother's Day – and families are feasting and celebrating here. Whew! I am happy we ordered a hotel a few weeks ago!

Our room is on the second floor, and when we open the door, we are amazed that the entire one side of the room is a window. This presents gorgeous scenery of powerful palm trees and just beneath us is a sparkling waterway lined with drinking birds.

From Margaret:

May 13:

I am at the Double Tree by Hilton Hotel Alice Springs and it is Mothers Day.

I think of the deep link and transfer of energy from generation to generation. The passing of love from ancestors to present day people, reflecting the gift of Love and Life of Mother Earth to her inhabitants.

I think of layers of history -- geologic and human. Time smooths harsh edges, dark patches. Peace will prevail. I think of the divine mission of the angels who tend to Mother Earth. Because today is Mother's Day, I particularly acknowledge the Divine Feminine giving birth to form. Thank you, Mother Earth, on Mother's Day.

Barbara comments:

We all came from off world. New ones are coming from off world to assist Mother Earth. The Aborigine Spirits will show/teach how to take care of the planet. Mother Earth is the ground base for many life forms.

More from Margaret:

Earlier, at the Outback Pioneer Hotel in Ayers Rock, I am pleased we have delivered to staff a message of our Love and Gratitude to Aborigine people who tendered and cared for this land.

I receive channeling:

The planet is sacred. The land is sacred. Life is sacred. Live life with that in mind.

The Aborigines paint in dots. This is energy painting. We are energy painting in words which is a point in time when we are giving love to the Earth, to each other, to humans, to birds, to sea creatures, to the Milky Way Galaxy.

Again from Margaret:

I think of the kangaroo whose tail is for balance and to help spring into action. Knowing this helps keep my mind positive for positive action of kindness, compassion, and helping. The kangaroo tail helps the heart to be positive.

I am thinking of the sweet birds that came to greet us at the Ayers Rock Outback Hotel. Are they Aborigines in bird form?

Now, from the Double Tree Hotel window, I put my mind on hundreds of birds that Barbara and I see coming with the setting of the sun. We think they are green parrots coming to roost for the night in a large eucalyptus tree across from our room. Each bird finds his/her own special branch for the night. Bird Land! In Australia, birds are so connected to humans, they catch my thoughts of enthusiasm, wonder and delight.

As we watch birds coming in and settling, I wonder how the tree can hold them all. Later, when I ask a hotel staff member about this, he says the hotel is like a zoo with parrots, squirrels and a peacock. How special! What a magnificent hotel!

I ponder on Alice Springs and I know there is great complexity here. Great power here. Artisan waters are under the ground. The power of Uluru and Kata Tjuta is direct and stands before the viewer, but the power of Alice Springs is hidden underground. Currents of life -- water -- is hidden beneath the surface. It is another energy system of vast power, hard to discern. Yet, I accept it will be revealed.

This area is dry on the surface but underneath flows powerful liquid water, clear and clean. Life force water. Water, the pure, pure element that can change mountains and create gorges.

Yes, I will focus on the water. I draw three Star Symbols connected to water -- Movement and Balance, Nature, and Protection of Nature to protect and honor water.

Love directs and high energy is received.

AUM.

From Barbara

May 14:

After a good night's sleep in Alice Springs, we have a free breakfast and we are ready to go to Corroboree Rock with a driver who will take us from 9 a.m. to 12 noon.

What is the importance of this place?

It is a site of an earth energy project that uses about sixteen places around the world to connect with each other on a common basis. Corroboree Rock is one of these places. A few years ago, people connected to the project understood the importance of Corroboree Rock, and they were expected to go there at a specific time to do ceremony. But they could not. They were ill.

Because we were coming to Australia, Margaret and I decided to go there with three small crystals and place them at the base of the Rock as a gesture of completion. And so, we have brought with us three tiny crystals.

We wished that these crystals had nothing in common with each other, and we have put them together so they would 'know' each other. Since all have a consciousness, including crystals, we knew they would quickly know each other.

In any case, Margaret and I are ready at 9 a.m. today to go to Corroboree Rock with the three tiny crystals in our pockets. A male tour leader, John Stafford, will take us in his car.

And yes, we soon realize John Stafford knows a lot about Australia. Along the way, to expand on what the road engineer woman told me earlier, I ask him why the desert around us is so bright red, and he says it is because of the iron in the mountains. The weathering of iron-bearing minerals because of oxidation gives the outer layer of rock a reddish brown color.

John Stafford tells us the names of Australian birds that have bright red breasts and he tells us that red kangaroos are very big and fat.

I mention I have seen evidence of fire, and he explains it was the custom earlier to burn land. But now that is discouraged because fire can go completely out of control and damage vegetation.

When we reach Corroboree Rock, I see the structure of the rock is EXTRAORDINARY. It looks as if many, many rocks have fallen on each other and yet they have not broken.

I feel the extraordinary power of the Aborigines, called here the Eastern Arrernte people, and I can hardly walk.

The Eastern Arrernte tell me, "We are charmed that you have come".

This startles me and I am especially caught on their word, "charmed".

Why have they used this word? It is not common. Ah, yes, I understand. They want me to remember they have spoken to me. And so, for me to remember, they have used an uncommon word.

My mind feels hundreds, thousands here. I begin meditating, and this meditation is so strong, I can feel hundreds, thousands doing their ceremonies.

Yes, they have lived a long time on this planet. I can understand why they do ceremony at this extremely powerful energy place.

I put down the three crystals Margaret and I have brought here. When doing this, the energy shakes me to the bone.

From Margaret:

May 14:

5:05 a.m., I am in the bedroom of the Double Tree Alice Springs Hotel, and I get up early to see if the birds are still in the great tree. I do not see them. There is a feeling of early dawn, but the night is still present. I know we are experiencing predawn energy when the birds and bird-like people stir to greet the new day.

I bring out the Vortexes to focus on the entire area – the underground water here, the massive stone formations, the mountain ridges. Raw land.

I think of the Aborigines who play their instrument called the didgeridoo. It is made of Mother Earth material and its sound directly addresses and reflects the heart frequency of Mother Earth.

I draw in the air and on my pad the twenty-two Star Law Symbols to focus especially on the Universal Law of Light, Sound and Vibration, the Universal Law of Love and the Spiritual Law of Healing.

Later, at breakfast in the hotel restaurant, we watch from the window a peacock enjoying the morning sun while preening his beautiful feathers. I go outside and try to capture his picture, but he knows how to elude intruding photography. He continues to go about his business and I take many shots but do not capture his full form and essence. Wise peacock. He will show off when he wants to show off. I smile. I have received his message.

After breakfast, we go to the front desk to confirm our reservation with John Stafford of Alice Springs Expeditions* who will take us for a half-day to Corroboree Rock. We have received his name from the Alice Springs Visitor Information Center.*

*See Glossary: Alice Springs Expeditions and Alice Springs Visitor Information Center.

John Stafford arrives at 9:00 a.m. with his English Land Rover that gives good comfort and good visibility.

To reach Corroboree Rock, he drives us on Ross Highway and we are passing gorges where streams millions of years ago have cut through the mountain ridges. Often these cuts are now used for roads.

As we move along, we find him to be kind, attentive and enthusiastic. He has great knowledge of trees, parrots and all sorts of birds. He tells us about the deep Artisan water underground, streams and rivers on the surface, the formation of the mountains and different rock layers.

At one place, John Stafford stops the Land Rover to show how water erosion cuts through mountains to make steep passes. These mountains look like caterpillars from the air, he says. The mountains are named for the caterpillars.

I speak of my fascination for underwater sea deposits in Australia because ancient seas once covered this area and that is why so much salt remains.

We also discuss parrots roosting at night in the Ghost Gum trees, and he tells us some trees shut off parts of their limbs to conserve water for the whole tree. Parts die to be rebuilt again and the holes are left for parrots to nest.

The history of the name Alice Springs has interest to me as well as the importance of telegraph building up and down the country.

At one point, John Stafford is curious why we are going to Corroboree Rock and Barbara tells him we want to place crystals at this sacred place.

He says Corroboree Rock is 800 million years old and the adjacent land is 350 million years old. The name means Gathering for Ceremony, and it is a very sacred place for the Aborigines.

When we arrive, my eyes stare at the POWERFUL rock formation. The whole area is POWERFUL.

Barbara puts down the three crystals here and before she begins meditating, she tells me the Aborigines want me to do the Vortexes.

I walk a bit with John to put down the Vortexes but I am hesitant at first to draw them because I do not wish to disturb the land. Then, when I enter a dry creek bed, I feel I can give the gift here and I draw with my finger the Sacred Symbols on a recording rock. While drawing, I speak the names of the Symbols and Vortexes. I feel overwhelmed.

The recording rock takes the Symbols and I know that when the creek/river flows again, the Symbols will travel with the water.

I feel a deep connection to the Star People who gave humanity the gift of the Symbols and to the ancient people who knew so well the stars and galaxies.

I feel blessed.

Then John tells me to look up to the birds in the sky. I look up and see two silver birds flying high. The sun catches their wings as they fly higher and higher, and then they disappear into the blue! Spirit Birds! I feel theses are spirit birds.

As we return to Barbara, we talk about the closeness of the stars here. We also speak about the passing on of the sacred traditions from older generations to the next.

When we reach Barbara, she says the ancient Aborigines told her they are enchanted that she has come so far to be with them.

AUM.

Now, John begins returning us to Alice Springs. Along the way, he tells us the Aborigines believe an individual born here is of the land and does not own the land. The land owns the people. One should stay where one is born. To the Aborigines, it is strange why people travel to live away from where they were born. Traditional Aborigines stay in one place and hold traditions. Other people from other cultures, he says, belong to Alice Springs if they were born here.

John asks us what do we want to do next and we answer we want to be with present-day Aborigines. So he returns us to Alice Springs where he places us in a busy supermarket in the middle of a mall flowing with people.

Later, he returns us to the hotel and we are very pleased with our morning expedition.

Now we eat and rest and wait for the parrots to come and roost for the night. Hundreds come. They feel our presence and we send them our love and greetings.

Also from Margaret:

Corroboree Rock is nothing like I have seen anywhere on Earth. Pure power energy of Mother Earth.

Later in the night, I receive the following channeling:

Now, Margaret, you have come to this sacred land and seen the power and received the power for yourself. You moved in and out of the landscape and have been changed by the encounter -- to see the most ancient rock, to know the stability and balance of the planet -- shown here in its un-tampered state.

This is a glorious radiant Star.

Mother Earth is full of wonders. Luckily, most of Australia's interior land is left alone. A blessing. There are some small towns, some roads, but the rest — the desert, rocks, mountains, dry streambeds that may flood once in eighteen months are left alone.

The Great Artisan water flows from North to South below ground. The folded mountains run from East to West. For eons of years, water has been cutting through the hard rock to form canyons and gaps. Sacred water. Sacred land. Sacred air. Sacred elements that keep it all running.

I receive another channeling:

What is so powerful here is that everything is on the surface and everything is hidden. When the eyes see through the heart lens, then everything is revealed -- the depth of time that lifts up and carves away mountains on this living, breathing, loving light shining planet star. Star people arrive, live and return, carrying the pollen of memories and frequencies as they travel.

You come to help the inhabitants now on this planet to transition to higher dimensions. Mother Earth is here waiting for her inhabitants to join her. The Aborigines are already with her in essence -- linked to the earth -- Mother Earth -- the nurturer -- the changer. Layers and layers of unseen helpers hold the form and spirit in place. This is boldly presented in the desert -- the ranges -- the Corroboree Rock projection. Power. It is its own telegraph station -- network -- channel -- portal -- presence to the other worlds and dimensions.

Thank you for the Vortexes -- the gift you were to bring with love.

With love from the Guardians of this land. As you travel forward, your thoughts will return you to here. A ticket back always is in the heart mind pocket.

Also from Margaret:

The next day, when we are ready to fly to Japan, we see reddish pink parrots flying, saying good-bye to us.

I know the birds have been living here a long, long time and they have no fear of modern humanity. They easily appear suddenly in front of us, fly by us, greeting us with song.

CHAPTER 5

Japan Journey Begins

From Barbara:

May 15:

Today we will go to Alice Springs Airport to leave Australia and go to Tokyo. We know it will take us a long time. Now, we must continue our day in Australia by going to the dining room of our hotel, the Double Tree, where we will eat a splendid breakfast. From the buffet, we select from five types of fruit, and of course we also take a glass of orange juice rather than water. I think I mentioned before that we have to pay for water. In our room, we have bottled water supplied by the hotel and we pay four dollars per bottle to drink it. One has to realize that we are in a desert country and so water is valuable.

After breakfast we check out of the hotel to take a shuttle bus to the airport. This bus ride is quick and we are soon at the airport and on a plane taking us to Sydney where we will transfer to a flight bound for Japan.

I sit at the window looking down at Australia, and I see desert, desert, desert, a land of sparse civilization although I know Aborigines once lived here in abundance. Many still live here. The color of the land is red and I remember the explanation about iron and rust. It isn't that the land has the same features everywhere. No. There are ridges and mounds and mountains and flat, flat, flat.

When we reach Sydney, I see this city spread out all over the place. Many, many houses and some green places for playing sports. I think Sydney looks like an interesting place to live.

When the pilot lands, we have a surprise. The plane for Japan does not leave in the same area. We are happy when an airport employee puts us in a car and drives us a long way to the terminal where we will take the Tokyo flight.

It is 5 p.m. when we reach this terminal and we have until 8 p.m. to board the plane for Tokyo. We note there are no waiting passengers and not even airport personnel. At first we are uncertain we are waiting in the correct place for our flight.

For a time, we sit patiently watching two little children playing with each other, racing here and there. Then, people begin to sit in our area. When more and more sit in our area, we feel confident we are waiting in the right place for our plane. Finally, an announcement for our flight is given, and we, along with about two hundred other passengers, board a flight to Tokyo.

They are pleasant and patient and their minds seem complex. I note that many have Japanese features, and I think they are returning home. When all passengers are seated for the flight, the pilot begins moving us slowly down the runway. Then the plane begins to move faster and faster until, with a mighty roar, it lifts off and we are in the air!

I look down from my window seat and I am amazed at the modern development of this huge city called Sydney that is in a country that has so much desert. Soon the stewards bring food for us, and after eating, I close my eyes and sleep. Others sleep, too. The plane is quiet.

May 16:

When I wake, there is bright sunshine. I have slept all night! And, the sunshine brings me relief. My worry has been that the plane will arrive at 5:15 a.m. and it will be so dark, one would have to be careful not to slip when walking. Well, there is no problem. The sun is shining brightly.

On arrival at Haneda Airport, Tokyo, two airport employees help us with our baggage as we walk what feels like a half mile to reach the customs people. And, there are many people waiting in line for their baggage to be examined. We join them and wait patiently for our baggage to pass inspection.

Outside the terminal building, a taxi driver takes us about two miles to the TamaDear Hotel, our first residence in Japan. When we reach it, we enter a comfortable-looking hotel and we are given room 505. Then we have breakfast.

From Margaret:

May 16:

After breakfast, we phone Hideo Nakazawa to tell him we have arrived in Japan. We laugh and he laughs when we realize this is the normal time when we daily reach him by SKYPE from the United States to pray for world peace.

Hideo knows we are here to give a talk focusing on our book, Healing By Contacting Your Cells.* He will be translating for the audience when we speak in two days in Shibuya, a popular, active commercial area of Tokyo.

*See Glossary: Healing By Contacting Your Cells.

Now we rest for a time until I go across the street to grocery shop in a little store that has beautiful selections of food. I buy yogurt, nuts, rolls, orange juice and berry juice, water, and dark chocolate.

We have the afternoon to ourselves and we decide to focus on what has been bothering us -- radiation in the sea and land of Japan since the nuclear accident in 2011. Now, in meditation we put this radiation into an esoteric container and send it to the sun with the expectation that the sun will return it as Love and Healing for Mother Earth.

From Barbara:

May 17:

This morning we work on our talk for tomorrow, and after the noon hour, we put our attention on Masami Kichimi who arrives in the early afternoon. He wants to hear our talk tomorrow, but he is unable to attend. And so, by previous arrangement, he will come to our hotel now.

By email, we have told him about a shrine near the hotel called the Anamori Inari Shrine which we learn has sacred sand. We do not know the significance of the shrine, but we would like to visit this place.

Masami Kichimi agrees to take us and when he arrives by taxi we are soon on our way to the sacred shrine.

From the taxi window, I watch as the driver maneuvers us through extensive traffic. Many people are walking beside the road. Yes, we are in an active part of Tokyo.

Soon Masami Kichimi announces we are at the shrine. Really? I only see tall, nondescript business buildings going up and up and up. As we exit the taxi, I realize the Anamori Inari Shrine is squashed in with these nondescript buildings. The shrine is only fifteen feet from one of them.

I walk onto the grounds of the shrine and I feel a sadness here. The guardian, a female Goddess, is sad. Well, I can certainly understand.

The only people here are two women sitting on a bench and talking. Then a businessman enters where they are sitting, takes out a cigarette, lights it and begins smoking. Has he come here to think of the Goddess? Are the gossiping women thinking of the Goddess?

I learn an interesting fact. The shrine was near Tokyo's Haneda Airport until after World War II when General Douglas MacArthur decided that Haneda Airport needed to be extensively enlarged. The Goddess was removed.

When I return home from our current Japan visit, I write to friends living in Japan to explain that I found the Goddess to be sad. Almost immediately, I receive a reply that there are other sad Goddesses throughout Japan and they are given prayers.

On return to the TamaDear Hotel, we sit in the dining area drinking peach soda and talking with Masami Kichimi. We learn he is a chiropractor by profession and his interests are in both Tokyo and Los Angeles. When we talk of concern for nuclear radiation in Japan, he is very interested. We tell him our talk tomorrow will include information on using Agnihotra, a method proved effective in reducing radiation poisoning. We promise to send him more information.

From Margaret:

When we are with Masami Kichimi at the shrine, he takes us through the tunnel of red gates to see the building containing healing sand. We are pleased when he gives us a gift of this sacred sand.

Later, Barbara makes a comment that her impression was that the Goddess of the shrine is sad because she did not want to leave Haneda Airport where she welcomed those who came and went. She was very active at the airport. Now, at her site away from the airport, she is among faceless skyscrapers and people coming to smoke and talk.

We know karma is here and we want to cancel the karma. When we return to the U.S.A., I ask for channeling and I receive:

Place the packets of sand with the Vortexes and link these to other sacred places such as Mount Fuji, Mount Shasta, Uluru, Denali. The sand contains crystals. Enliven the crystals. Perhaps place the crystal packet in your StarGate with the Vortexes and play the 10,000 Ode to Joy so these crystal sands can send to the Brothers and Sisters (crystals) Light, Sound and Vibration, Love, and Healing of that musical performance of hope, healing and joy from Japan to the world.

After receiving the channeling, we put sacred sand from the shrine in our hands and we listen to Beethoven's Ode to Joy being sung by 10,000 joyous Japanese voices.* We know this makes a difference because earlier it made a difference.

*See Glossary: 10,000 singing Ode to Joy.

One time, when we spoke by SKYPE to Hideo Nakazawa of Japan, we told him we had listened in the morning to 10,000 Japanese singing Ode To Joy. We were surprised when he told us an earthquake had hit Japan in the afternoon. Later, when I channeled the Higher Worlds, I was told the music of 10,000 people singing Ode to Joy had reduced the power of the earthquake that struck in the afternoon.

Now I want to return to our conversation with Masami Kichimi after we leave the Anamori Inari Shrine. He tells us he was born and raised near Fukushima and he lost family members as a result of the 2011 earthquake that brought radiation to Japan. He is concerned about radiation.

We explain about the Agnihotra Fire that reduces radiation and we give him an article, the Scientific Aspects of Agnihotra Fires.* We promise to send him more material.

*See Glossary: Scientific Aspects of Agnihotra.

It is late afternoon when Masami Kichimi leaves and before he leaves, he tells he has read our book, Healing By Contacting Your Cells. That is why he wanted to meet us.

After Masami Kichimi leaves, Barbara and I want to meditate to lessen energetically the radiation in Japan and the Pacific. I want to use the Vortexes to do this. Then the Higher Worlds tell me to use the Vortexes in reverse order, and so I begin with the Spiritual Law of Healing, then Love, then Protection of Nature, and Nature. This is the first time I have ever reversed the Vortexes and the Symbols. I feel they appear to be in a more protective stance.

CHAPTER 6

Our Talks in Shibuya (Tokyo)

From Barbara:

May 18:

Today will be a BIG DAY, a very complicated day. We need to keep our spirits positive with smiles on our faces. We will give our talk in Shibuya, an extensive area of hustle and bustle in Tokyo.

First, we need to go to Haneda Airport in order to go to Shibuya. Then, after we reach the airport, we must ask for help on how to reach Shibuya. FORTUNATELY at the airport we are told in English where to buy a shuttle bus ticket to Shibuya and where to wait for the bus.

As we are waiting inside the terminal, we watch Japanese women wearing flamboyant dresses, and some are wearing high heels. Also, some are wearing interesting makeup. The men are not as well presented as the women.

Finally, we realize we need to wait outside the building for the bus. And yes, this is a good choice because here are lighted signs telling us which buses are coming. The signs are updated continually as we watch the coming and going. When our bus arrives, we take a seat just behind the driver. We tell him in English that we want to get off at a place called The Meeting Place in Shibuya and he nods his head in understanding. Three stops, he tells us in English.

Then he smartly and expertly begins driving and we sit behind him looking at busy Tokyo streets. As we are moving along, after about fifteen minutes, I begin looking for a Shibuya sign. And yes, I do see a Shibuya road sign both in Japanese and in English. We go along a bit more and suddenly the bus driver makes a sharp left turn into a huge parking garage and continues up a ramp! When he stops the bus, are we to get off? He motions for us to remain seated.

Other people get off the bus and the driver begins his journey down the ramp. But, we see Mieko Sakai.

"Hellooooo, Mieko!"

The bus stops and we get off and hug each other.

WHAT A RELIEF to see her!!

From Margaret:

Mieko Sakai, who found a location for our talks, has given us instructions on how to reach her. We know we are to leave the International Haneda Airport Terminal at 12:15 p.m. on an airport limousine bus that will arrive at the Shibuya Excel Hotel at 1:37 p.m. She will pick us up at the hotel and take us to The Meeting Room where we will be speaking.

When we leave the airport, the bus driver takes us through a complex river port area and then we pass tall business buildings that are modern and non-descript except for the Japanese Eiffel Tower and a huge Ferris Wheel. Many buildings are built on top of buildings. There are a few old holdouts where a modern building had to be built around a low, older building.

As we approach Shibuya, the area is more and more dense. Big, busy, hurry, hurry. Young business people scrambling. We make our way through great jams of traffic, stopping at each light. I know we are on the right bus to meet Mieko Sakai so I mostly relax until we reach the Excel Hotel Tokyu when the driver abruptly turns off the road and begins driving up a ramp. When he stops at the 5th floor parking level, we look out the bus window and see Mieko. Wonderful!!!

We get off the bus and she guides us to The Meeting Room Building where a room has been rented for us to speak this afternoon in less than an hour. Just before meeting us, Mieko unlocked the door, which is coded. Now, when she is with us and trying to open the door, it will not open! OH DEAR! Well, a phone call to the superintendent in charge of the locked door brings success, and we are soon entering a room filled with chairs. Quickly, we begin to arranging them for our audience.

Hideo Nakazawa arrives and he will translate our talks. Hiro Kawagishi comes with a kora, a large African stringed instrument that he will play. Within minutes, guests begin arriving. Everyone is jovial and smiling and smiling. Mitsuru Ooba, who films events, begins photographing. Everything is ready.

At 3:00 p.m. Hiro opens the session by playing his music on the kora. Then we begin our talks, paragraph by paragraph, and Hideo translates paragraph by paragraph. The audience is very attentive. Many are holding our book in their hands.

———————

From Barbara:

Here is my talk:

Margaret and I have written a book, Healing By Contacting Your Cells, which is a quick, easy-to-read, email-style book to find a way to cure Margaret's cancer signals that were not responding to standard or alternative medical treatments.

We had no maps to show us roads that would lead us to success, but we were determined to find a successful completion to our journey. We had only our intuition to guide us.

Well, we tried this road and we tried that road, and gradually we began to feel encouraged, hopeful that we would have a successful ending.

And yes, we did succeed! Margaret's cancer signals went away. We think our book can be viewed as a road map with pointers that can be used to create spiritual journeys for others with similar disease problems.

I tell Margaret that LOVE is the key word for healing. She has a factory of cells and the factory is there for her. It is her sacred temple. This sacred temple was given to her so she could be here on this earth at this time.

I tell Margaret she needs to do a good cleaning of her sacred temple, her factory, starting with the attic and gathering all the junk up there and giving it a big toss into the factory trash container.

I tell Margaret over and over again, she must love her factory of cells. They are required to be with her every day. Day after day after day. And they must tolerate her thoughts of love and non-love. They cannot leave to live in another dimension. They are here with her to do the job of providing her with a sacred temple.

I also tell Margaret that her factory of cells loves her anyway, no matter how much she neglects them with non-love.

I want to speak here about blockages and cement that play a role in forming disease. It is my understanding that fingers and toes at the end of a body are like leaves at the end of limbs. If a tree is not treated properly, the leaves at the end of the tree begin to show suffering.

It is the same with a human body. Mistreatment will cause blockages in the system. Worry and fear and improper care can be the reason for dis-ease in the body.

Improper eating can cause cement in the stomach, and this will hinder the service work of the other cells in the body.

Blockages and cement hold toxins not only from food but from worry and fear thoughts manufactured by thoughts presented by television or strangers or acquaintances. All this resides in the stomach along with food cement.

When cell roadways within the body are blocked from pileups, cement, they become sluggish and congested. What happens when these roadways are finally cleared enough for normal service goods to get through? Moving has become laced with toxins and poisons that reach the end rooms of the factory -- the fingers and toes. Hence, inflammation -- disease.

For those who know nothing about cell factories and blockages and poison buildups, when dis-ease occurs and they need to be treated, the usual procedure is to give pills.

But, pills are not natural substances for the factory of cells to handle. And so, even though pills may help reduce the disease, in the long run, the cell factory often becomes overloaded with unnatural stuff and so more and more cells have to be taken off their normal jobs to handle this. Hence, other places become short-staffed. And so, the cells systems begin to suffer even more. The factory is in even worse disarray. A vicious cycle.

How much easier would it be to attend to the source of the problem so the cells are free and clear of toxins and poisons that lead to disease.

Remember LOVE is a great healer.

I think that many, many disease sufferers remain as sufferers because they are not asked to change their habits and clean out their factories, and they do not know the power of LOVE.

I conclude my talk with the following:

If you have a body problem, Margaret and I hope that our book, Healing By Contacting Your Cells, will be helpful to you.

From Margaret:

Here is my talk to the audience at The Meeting Room.

For two years I used standard and alternative medical treatments to heal a bladder problem. But, for some reason my body refused to heal. Barbara said this problem could develop into full-blown cancer.

She told me that the Native Americans have a common spiritual saying, 'All Our Relations', which refers to the relations in ALL families. This means the family of cells in our bodies, the family called flowers, trees, rocks, Mother Earth, and even our sun. To the Native American, all are ONE. All are alive. All have a consciousness.

Barbara said we can judge the truth of this belief that all have a consciousness by probing our intuition. If our intuition says 'yes, correct', then we can proceed until the assumption is proven otherwise.

I agreed with this belief and I was full of hope. I was ready to proceed.

I opened Gray's Anatomy to locate the position of the bladder in my body and I visually studied it. I addressed the cells and told them I loved them. I know they have traveled with me to different places. I asked them where would they like to go.

They chose the singing program in Samoa in the Pacific where we had been before. They knew the music and loved the music so they were comfortable going there. I gave them love. Interestingly, I realized I gave them attention and love but I did not ask them what was the matter. Oh dear!

Then the cells spoke, *"Love heals"*.

Later, in meditation, I was with the orchids and I gave them love and I could even smell their presence. I asked what was wrong with the cells and I was told the cells were affected by fear, anger, and judgment.

I remembered driving past beautiful pastures, looking longingly at cows peacefully eating. The cows were not worried about anything. They were happily eating. I realized that man holds worries even when eating. Animals do not.

So here was the key – worry. I understood I had to give up holding onto what was happening in the world today – the frustration and sadness. It becomes like cement in one's system, hard to eliminate. I knew I had to lighten up and remove cement from my old thought patterns of anger, resentment, judgment. When negative talk comes to me, I must transform it into fertilizer for the trees that feed the animals and birds.

Now, in meditation, the orchids showed my cells a perfect balance structure of all being in harmony. They gave their love to the cells. They heard my request for healing and they gave their strength and love.

Then I asked my cells, what are cells, and they answered:

Building blocks, fluid exchanges, balancing agents. Cells bring Light. Cells bring energy. They carry nutrients, carry off toxins, create walls, expand, divide. Cells are adaptable. They communicate with one another. One consciousness.

There is more:

They love the body temperature – not too hot – not too cold. They are ageless – young, old, the same. They can hear. They can sense. Cells like freedom and order like a happy, harmonious factory that is fully functioning. No angry thinking. Worry, as well as thoughts of conflict and shock, needs to be sliced. When there is shock, they try to compress, distort, run away.

All cells feel patience, happiness, joy. They respond to the positive or negative vibration of reading or writing. They like quiet or soft speaking.

My cells tell me they respond to All That IS – Love frequency and Harmony.

When our talks end, we ask for questions and there are many. During a break, many approach us asking to sign our books.

From Barbara:

For the second part of our afternoon session, we intend to focus on the use of Agnihotra to help reduce radiation affecting Japan because of the nuclear accident several years ago. First we show an Agnihotra fire demonstration video* and Hideo translates.

*See Glossary: Agnihotra video.

Earlier, we gave him an article on research showing how Agnihotra affects the environment for the good by causing a diminishing of radioactivity.* In Japanese, Hideo presents this to the audience.

*See Glossary: Scientific Aspects of Agnihotra.

Everyone listens attentively as he speaks and we watch the concern on their faces. We realize we need to continue addressing this concern.

At 5:00 p.m. when the meeting is over, we go next door with many in the group to a restaurant where we have spaghetti and honey tea. Then Margaret and I spend two plus hours relaxing while Hiro Kawagishi skillfully drives us to his home. We will be staying with him throughout the remainder of our journey in Japan.

CHAPTER 7

Countryside of Japan, Chiba

From Barbara:

May 18:

After completing our talks at The Meeting Room in Shibuya, Hiro Kawagishi begins driving us to his house in Chiba near the coastline south of Tokyo. This will be our nest until we leave Japan on May 22.

At first he drives us through heavily congested Tokyo, but as we move closer to his Chiba home, the congestion is less. Skyscrapers are behind us, and we cross a big river.

On and on we go, and we begin seeing houses among trees and green rice fields. In fact, we see a lot of green rice fields. It looks as if grass is being grown, but we know it is rice that the people will eat. The multitude of rice fields makes me realize that MANY, maybe ALL of the Japanese eat rice as their predominant food source.

When we arrive at Hiro's house, it is within a forested area with many, many, green, healthy-looking, big trees.

As is the custom, we take off our shoes at the front entrance and put on slippers waiting for us. Now we enter a magnificent kitchen which we remember from two years ago when we stayed at Hiro's house.

And yes, we know how to reach our sleeping quarters. We open a kitchen door and walk straight ahead before turning left and walking a short way to the closed, sliding doors of our sleeping quarters.

Hiro immediately begins fixing supper for us, and he is out of the house several times to pick plants to be added to his cooking.

Dinner and then to bed for me. I am tired! This has been a big day!

From Margaret:

The drive takes over two hours and on arrival at Hiro's farmhouse, he fixes dinner for us. Then, after dinner, Barbara goes to bed and Hiro and I talk about all sorts of things. He tells me he is rebuilding his house in a traditional way – with traditional natural materials from the land.

He says young people are interested in returning to the traditional ways of following non-consumerism. For example, they want to learn how to make soy sauce in ancient barrels as in the old way. They want to live simply and far from the hustle and bustle of Tokyo with rush, rush, rush, buy, buy, buy the latest fashion and cosmetics.

I go to bed at 11:30 p.m.

From Barbara:

May 19:

The day begins leisurely with Margaret and me putting our thoughts on the countryside with its large trees and some flowers. The weather is warm and there is a slight breeze. Hiro is again preparing breakfast for us in the kitchen, and he would rather do this himself. He makes us a vegetable salad and a tuna fish salad which is not a normal breakfast for me, but it is excellent!

When breakfast is over, Hiro drives us to a nearby shrine and we know this place well. In fact, on the wall near Margaret's computer in the U.S.A. is a picture of a giant tree earlier photographed at this shrine. We estimate the tree is 500 years old or more.

Why are we so interested in this shrine and tree?

A few years ago, when we visited, we went from the shrine to the Pacific Ocean which is only a few minutes away. Here, a young child was nearly drowned because of heavy wind and a pounding surf while we were doing esoteric matters. Then the wind stopped abruptly and the surf subsided. The child was saved.

We felt the shrine and the tree had much to do with saving the child's life. And so, we have returned to the shrine to say 'hello' and to pat the big tree. Then we go to the Pacific Ocean beach.

Well, I am very surprised! The weather conditions today are exactly opposite the earlier wild time. There is no wind and the ocean waters are calm. In fact, because of the calm water, the beach itself seems to have grown at least five times larger.

No one except we three are on the beach.

From Margaret:

May 19:

Early in the morning, I wake to channel. I say, dear Higher Worlds, we are here in the sacred Chiba farmhouse of Hiro that is based on the old tradition of peace and harmony with Nature. We delight in the understanding of grace and proportion in the structure and design of this old house.

But, Barbara and I are worried about modern Japan. The 2011 Fukushima radiation event affects the environment. Should we speak about our concern?

I am answered: *Continue on your lines of thoughts. You have the enthusiastic interest in the Agnihotra Fires. Let what is not talked about be talked about - to insure a way of life for the people and for Nature. Address the concern with a creative solution. That is all you need. We support your efforts.*

From the Higher Worlds.

At 7:00 a.m. I hear sweet classical music broadcast to the area. I know this is a tradition to wake the people in a pleasant way. I hope this continues.

We greet Hiro as he is fixing breakfast for us and again he does not want us to help. He is combining chopped vegetables with tuna and cabbage, leeks, bread and butter and oil, fermented orange and yogurt and special tea. Delicious!

While eating breakfast, I can see the trees outside and they are happy. They know we want to bring the teachings of the sacred Agnihotra fire to reduce radiation. The trees themselves will benefit and so will the rice fields, soil and everything else.

After breakfast, we go to the nearby ancient shrine we visited a few years ago. As we approach, we see the statues of temple guardian lions. At the top of the steps we acknowledge not one but two ancient trees.

Then we look to the left and see a massive ancient tree that reminds me of Corroboree Rock!! Two separate trees have merged into one. Birds are pointing out its location, acknowledging its power, and we feel it is one thousand years old. We greet the great tree and honor it.

Now we drive to Ubara Beach with its delicate cove and natural bridge. We were here two years ago to give the gift of the Vortexes for the healing of the ocean. It was here where the child was saved at the last moment.

At the water's edge, I use a stick to draw the Vortex Symbols and the waves come in to take them. Large, hawk-like birds fly close to acknowledge what I am doing. I draw the twenty-two Symbols. I find special at this time and place the Symbols of Spiritual Freedom, Symmetry, and Change.

The wind picks up appearing to focus on the Symbols of Life, Nature, Love, and Healing. I witness the wind and the birds creating one, two, three, four circles of greetings to acknowledge the gift of the Symbols. A large bird of prey, similar to a hawk or eagle, flies directly over the drawn Symbols, and Hiro tells me the bird is a Tombi. Here Nature has received the gift.

As we are returning to the car, two butterflies circle and spin. They are Guardians of the Vortex of Change.

From Barbara:

Now Hiro has a suggestion. He wants to take us to a nearby restaurant to feed us soba and tempura. What is that, I ask in ignorance, and he answers that soba are cooked noodles made of buckwheat flour and tempura are fried shrimp and battered vegetables deep fried. The restaurant is not far away, he says, hoping we will want to go.

Yes, of course, let us go, we answer him without knowing exactly what to expect.

Well, the soba and tempura are excellent!

He tries to teach me how to properly eat noodles by using my chopsticks to quickly put the noodles to my mouth. When they reach my mouth, I must make a big SLURP as they go in.

I try unsuccessfully for a time, especially while making the Slurp sound, but once I am able to make the sound, he is satisfied.

When we leave the restaurant, we stop at an ice cream place for American-style dessert.

Yes, we have a humorous time with Hiro.

CHAPTER 8

Symphony Of Peace Prayers, Mount Fuji

From Barbara:

May 20:

Yearly, on May 20, the SOPP, a Symphony of Peace Prayers event,* is celebrated in Japan to pay attention to the concept of The Fuji Declaration* which concentrates on the creation of a Divine Spark. It is believed that creating a Divine Spark will unite all humanity in recognizing the value and dignity of each and every life.

*See Glossary: Symphony of Peace Prayers.

*See Glossary: The Fuji Declaration.

A great many from around the world come to Japan to do this. They are of different religions and spiritual traditions and they come together to act as one.

Barbara Wolf & Margaret Anderson

Masami Saionji heads this effort, and on May 20 people gather outside her Fuji Sanctuary which is within the energy field of sacred Mount Fuji. For the ceremony, they seat themselves on vast green grounds to face an outdoor stage where the performance ceremony will be held.

From Margaret:

In an earlier book, I have put channeling from Saint Germain speaking about the importance of this May 20 event to help create a Divine Spark where all of humanity unites.

Channeling from Saint Germain:

Margaret, the earth is in a period of turmoil. Each country is facing its own political and environmental turmoil expressed in earthquakes, volcanoes, large storms, hurricanes, tornadoes. The people are very unsteady and agitated, reflecting the conditions on the planet. Which comes first – the peoples' agitation or the land's agitation? They are interchangeable.

Calm is needed. Balance is needed. Truth is needed. The gates between cultures need to be open and the moderate people need to communicate, exchange positive (love, light) frequencies for there to be peace and balance on the planet.

The Fuji Declaration takes the world agenda off focusing on religions to a more universal focus of cooperative human interaction based on the symbol of the mountain, Mount Fuji, which is balanced on all sides, soaring up to Heaven. The Nature world, Mount Fuji, is more stable than the human world. It is time for the perfection of Heaven to be reflected in perfection on earth.

The speaking now needs to be moderate, seeking harmony between people. Shocking confrontations create shockwaves that further destabilize the earth systems. The drumbeat of war, frequencies of

72

conflict, need to be turned down and peace frequencies, harmonies, cooperation need to be emphasized.

The Fuji document seeks to do this – to counterbalance the turmoil of Earth at this time. Turn down the fire of rhetoric. Turn up the frequencies of peaceful co-existence. If the 'co' is taken out, then there will be no existence on the planet.

Peace is of upmost importance.

Saint Germain

From Barbara:

Masami Saionji brings together on this day religious leaders of different faiths, Muslim, Christian, Jewish, etc. They stand on this outdoor stage to give their prayers to the vast audience which hold in their hands the prayers being said. They will repeat these prayers no matter what religion they themselves believe in. They will have the knowledge that everyone there, regardless of faith, will be repeating the prayers with them. This helps bring a powerful message of unity and harmony. And it helps establish the realization that people of different faiths can come together to build a peaceful world.

The May 20 Symphony of Peace Prayers also will display flags from every nation, and these flags will be individually recognized as equal to each other.

Sacred Mount Fuji will be in the background.

Yes, Margaret and I are eager to join the SOPP and so, at 5:00 a.m., on May 20, Hiro begins driving us to Mount Fuji for the ceremony. There has been some rain worry today but we see no evidence of rain. In fact, from time to time as we are riding along, the sun briefly comes out.

When we first see Mount Fuji, which is still far ahead of us, we see strips of snow on the mountain. As we come closer and closer to the mountain, I see more and more cars going in the same direction as we are going. Probably about three thousand people will attend this fantastic world gathering at the foot of the sacred mountain.

We arrive at the Mount Fuji Sanctuary at 9:15 a.m., one hour before the beginning of the ceremony, and already many people are here. We park and soon we are met by cheerful sanctuary helpers who take us to an outdoor viewing area where we can watch today's events.

We are treated as Guests of Honor which means we will be sitting on a raised platform looking down at an outdoor stage. The 3,000 sitting on the grass are below us, looking up to the outdoor stage.

When we arrive, other Guests of Honor are already seated on the raised platform. Diplomats from Syria will be sitting in front of us. We are all wearing artificial, big, white roses to indicate we are Guests of Honor.

When the program begins, the names of the Guests of Honor are individually spoken, and we stand for a moment to bow.

Now religious leaders are invited to the outdoor stage to speak their prayers, and the audience, in unison, repeats these prayers. This gives a strong feeling of unity, of family, which is the purpose of SOPP.

Flags are brought out -- all of them brought together -- and then individually recognized. None are regarded to be better than the other.

The program continues for a long time, and everyone seems happy and joyful to be here in this place of peace and harmony.

When the event ends and Hiro begins driving us in his car, we stop at a small restaurant to eat. Here, we meet two women who attended the SOPP event, and when we discover this, we sit with them and talk.

From Margaret:

When Hiro begins driving us from his house to attend the big ceremony called the Symphony of Peace Prayers, the early morning is clear with a bit of chill. I dress with many layers to keep warm, and I can take them off when the weather becomes warmer.

Specifically, along the way, I want to see Sacred Mount Fuji who will be overlooking the event.

Hiro drives us first through the countryside with rice fields, and then he drives through forests to reach the mountains. I connect these mountains with Australia, Shasta, and Hawaii because they have the same vibration as Lemuria, the civilization in the Pacific during ancient times. I feel the strength of these mountains holding the Pacific together.

Yes, I feel the power and grace of Lemuria. These mountains hold this power and send love and stability to the oceans and sea creatures. As Hiro drives, I send prayers to these mountains, to the land, to the trees, to the animals and sea creatures that are always nearby.

Hiro then drives us at sea level near a large industrial city close to the ocean and the mountains are no longer visible. After we leave the industrial area, I see the mountains again, and I feel these mountains are guardians of Mount Fuji.

Now I look for Mount Fuji, and yes, I see Mount Fuji sitting LARGE and POWERFUL, capped with long streaks of snow.

When we reach the grounds of Fuji Sanctuary, Mount Fuji faces us, open and accessible. Today is a gorgeous day. There is a feeling of great joy! It is a brilliant day with cool, bright, clear shining LIGHT.

Now, we make our way to the greeting tent where we each receive a beautiful white rose and a Guest of Honor label.

At a welcoming table we meet dear friends past and present. One of them is Mieko Sakai who arranged our speaking engagement two days ago, and another is Keiko Nakamichi who helped us during our visit to Hiroshima a few years ago.

We are taken to the seating area for Guests of Honor and the first two rows are for visiting religious leaders from around the world. We sit in the third row. When all the representatives of the different religions arrive, I am impressed they greet each other warmly, like old friends.

The program begins at 10:15 a.m. with Masami Saionji's powerful speech of greeting to the audience. Then we are asked to pray together and give prayers for peace in different languages and religions. I feel deep unity among the audience and the religious leaders.

When the World Peace Prayer Society Flag Ceremony begins, there is a magnificent presentation of the flags of the world. Everyone prays for peace in each country -- 193 countries. The ceremony is helped by the bright, intense light of the sun and Mount Fuji overlooking the event.

When the Symphony of Peace Prayers Ceremony ends, friends gather to take pictures.

Then Hiro begins driving us to his farmhouse, but his drive is different from earlier. Now we are in much traffic, and we are hardly moving, so we decide to stop at a restaurant to give time for the traffic to clear.

In the restaurant, we are seated at a table next to two ladies and we are amazed when we learn they were also at the Symphony of Peace Prayers. We begin talking with them and instead of staying a few minutes, we stay a long time at the restaurant.

When we begin our trip again to Hiro's home, we learn there has been an accident on the road that has stopped traffic. And so, Hiro suggests that we avoid the stopped traffic by taking a longer route home. He says this longer route will take us to sacred Mount Hakone and its hot springs. Yes, we want to see this mountain and its hot springs. It does not bother us if the route is long.

When we reach this mountain, it seems to me that Mount Hakone is as tall as Mount Fuji, but, in fact, Mount Fuji is much taller than Mount Hakone. However, I know there is a deep connection between Mound Hakone and Mount Fuji. I feel Mount Hakone is a Guardian of Mount Fuji.

A few years ago, I remember there were intense emissions from the steam vents of Mount Hakone and parts of the area were closed. Now everything is peaceful. In fact, we can see Mount Fuji directly from Mount Hakone.

What flashes in my mind is that Mount Fuji sits on the intersection of three tectonic plates and close to a fourth. Mount Fuji's presence holds the balance, the stability of this vital area of the meeting of tectonic plates.*

*See Glossary: Mount Fuji and tectonic plates.

We drive two more hours, which means that Hiro has been driving six plus hours to take us to his home.

I want to conclude my notes here by saying that over the years I have attended the Symphony of Peace Prayers and this one today is the best. The day has been filled with Light, joy, harmony and compatibility.

The field has been plowed and the seeds of Peace have been planted.

CHAPTER 9

Second Talk Session, Japan

From Barbara:

May 21:

Today, Monday, the morning starts leisurely after a good night's sleep. During breakfast, I ask Hiro to explain again his concept of living in a traditional Japanese farmhouse. He says, in ancient times, a house would feel like it was part of the outdoors. It was made of wood and its interior had no plastic or artificial materials. It was like the land of trees and Nature. Today, he is remodeling his house to fit this thought and he shows us examples of new/old walls.

Before noon, Hiro's wife Rei, who has been away, comes to the house for a special purpose. She will translate as Margaret and I talk to an audience of friends gathered at the house. Yes, we will be speaking again, and this time we will be speaking with their friends as well as neighbors.

Because our talks will be after lunch, we will have time in the morning to practice with Rei. When we begin practicing with her, we realize she is a professional translator. Her manner is relaxed and friendly and we feel relaxed and friendly with her. She advises us to go sentence by sentence rather than paragraph by paragraph for translation.

When the audience begins to come, they gather and are seated in an adjacent area of the house. Kind neighbors have brought additional chairs for all to be confortable. Some have come from as far away as Tokyo and Osaka. Our friend Mitsuru Ooba has come to film.

As all are seating themselves, Hiro begins playing his kora and then he plays his guitar until everyone is ready for our talks.

At 2:30 p.m. we begin speaking about our book, Healing By Contacting Your Cells. Each person has a copy in his hands and these have been translated and published in Japan.

They begin listening intently as we begin speaking. Rei does an excellent job of translating as we go sentence by sentence and phrase by phrase with emphasis and comments.

Hiro has arranged for a tea and cookie break and during this break, everyone comes to have our book signed.

What fun!

From Margaret:

Now we have a question and answer session and the main question is how to contact one's cells. I say to go into the body and appreciate the amazing working systems of the cells -- to visit their domain -- the brain, the eyes, the lungs, the heart, the liver, the stomach, legs, feet and toes. Each person needs to marvel at this amazing creation.

I say, imagine you have just landed from space and you are seeing your body for the first time. Your mind comprehends that this is where you have been living. Be pleased and observe and be happy. Step silently and give love and gratitude for the amazing gift of living in your body.

Everyone is interested and smiling and smiling. Barbara and I smile back.

During the break, a woman goes to the sacred tree area near the house and witnesses amazing shafts of Light. She catches this on her iPad and Mitsuru Ooba captures this picture with his camera.

Now, others tell very personal stories about healing, loss and recovery of joy after loss. Our hearts are singing in harmony. Everyone is having a wonderful time sharing love and gratitude and appreciating one another.

Yes, we are all one. This is an echo of the Symphony of Peace Prayers Ceremony we attended yesterday.

When it is time to leave, a group photograph is taken of everyone bubbling with happiness. Barbara and I are overjoyed.

From Barbara:

May 22:

Today is Tuesday, and Rei, Hiro's wife, tells us she is ready to go to Geneva, Switzerland to attend a conference on the abuse of women in the workplace. She will be there two weeks.

Margaret and I pack our bags and are ready to go with Hiro to the Narita Airport to begin flights to our country. But when we leave the farmhouse, we first stop at the shrine to say goodbye to the big tree.

I think of all the trees we have seen in Japan this year and I think of how big and healthy they look. My thought is that they are doing their job promoting oxygen for the air.

When our plane lifts off to take us from Japan to the U.S.A., I look down at Tokyo and I can hardly see it because of the pollution in the air. Yes, Japan needs big, healthy green trees to help counter the pollution.

From Margaret:

May 22:

6:00 a.m. I am up early writing by the window from which brings in a view of the Lumurian forest shining in the bright morning sun.

I sketch on my notepad a drawing of Mount Fuji and I feel that our days in Japan have been blessed. I feel the loving energy of Mount Fuji and the Symphony of Peace Prayers. Now I draw energy lines going out from Mount Fuji to the world.

7:00 a.m. we have breakfast with Hiro and his wife Rei who will be heading to Geneva, Switzerland for translation work.

Barbara and I are packed and ready to fly to the U.S.A., but first we stop at the sacred shrine to give our love and gratitude to the tall trees and to Nature. A great Grey Heron greets us. The tall trees greet us. The ancient double tree is there. I observe the intricate carvings of dragons, turtle and heron on the temple with the guarding lions at the gate. The temple bell waits to be rung for prayer. I feel the directional points of the ancient shrine sending Love and Power out to all Japan.

Now Hiro begins driving us to the airport and we see rice fields and forests. It is hard to leave this beautiful country.

When Hiro drops us off at the airport, we thank him one thousand fold for all he has done to make our journey a great delight.

Our plane, American Airlines, is big and comfortable, and soon we are ready to settle into our seats to begin dreaming about our wonderful journey.

CHAPTER 10

Australia 1989 Visit

We are ending this book by telling you about Barbara's visit to Australia in 1989 when Agnihotra, a healing method, was used. We think this method needs to be understood to help Japan be relieved of radiation acquired from the 2011 nuclear accident.

From Barbara:

The technique called Agnihotra has been with the public for years and years. In 1984, when a pesticide factory in India began releasing deadly toxic gases, many died from gas exposure. To purify the atmosphere, the technique of Agnihotra was used, and this proved to be successful. Newspapers published announcements about the positive affects, and a great many began to use the technique.

What is this technique?

Fires are burned in copper pyramids at sunrise and sunset and during the day. The sun has a place in this healing because its energies will purify at the same time as impurities are destroyed. Especially at sunrise is the sun important because it will send out powerful positive energies.

To augment healing energies, mantras are chanted.

We have mentioned Agnihotra several times in this book. You will find it mentioned in the Glossary.*

*See Glossary: Agnihotra.

I want to tell you that in 1989 I went to Ayers Rock with now-deceased Doreen Rajaloo of Ireland who was an expert on Agnihotra. We intended to perform Agnihotra at Ayers Rock, one of the most powerful places on this planet because its energy is joined with eleven other powerful locations around the world. By concentrating on one of them, Ayers Rock, we knew we were actually giving energy to all of them as well as to the whole world.

We preform Agnihotra at Ayers Rock on January 20, 1989, the moment of the full moon of Aquarius, a POWERFUL date.

The day before, January 19, when we fly over Australia to reach Ayers Rock, we look down at the vast countryside below us that was earlier inhabited almost entirely by Aborigines. Well, that has changed. The Aborigines now take second place to foreigners who came to live here.

When we arrive at Ayers Rock's small airport, it is hot, very hot. We have arrived during hot summer weather.

At the airport we take a bus driven by an Australian park ranger to the Yulara Tourist Resort, which, we understand, has the only accommodations for Ayers Rock. The entire area has been turned over to the Aborigines, and former tourist buildings have been torn down to bring the land to its former state.

From our air-conditioned bus we look out at the hot, hot countryside and we are surprised there is so much green amid the bright red sand of this area. The reason for the green, the driver tells us, is the amount of rain that has fallen. He says that in the past ten or eleven months, there has been more rain than the previous twenty-seven to twenty-eight years.

When we arrive at the Yulara Tourist Resort, we realize there are different types of accommodations here and we decide to rent a Maisonette. This Yulara Tourist Resort has every need available, such as shops for buying food and souvenirs, and there are restaurants. However, all are contained close together. Just outside this contained area is only Nature. Man is not allowed to disturb the land outside the confines of the resort area.

We put our luggage in our rented Maisonette, and we take a bus to Ayers Rock for sunset viewing. As the sun is dropping in the sky, we see the Rock is beginning to change to different shades of colors.

Doreen and I are dropped off at the place where tourists can begin climbing to the top of Ayers Rock. We think the slick red skin of this sacred place is more interesting to look at than climbing it.

We are feeling the magnetism of this place and we know that Ayers Rock is the magnetic center of the continent. The powerful energy is coming up our shoes, our feet, up into our bodies. At the bottom of this red-skinned marvel, we find a place to sit and take in the energy.

Sunset is coming and we watch the Rock beginning to change its red tones. In the distance, we see its sibling, the Olgas, and this sibling is not changing its colors too much. At sundown, Ayers Rock becomes grayish as if it has lost its aura, like an old being beginning to die.

We wake very early the next morning, January 20, first day of Aquarius, full moon, and we go outside to build an Agnihotra fire at dawn. We take our Agnihotra pot and the ingredients we need, and we walk down a stone path behind the Maisonette where we are staying to find a satisfactory place for building the fire.

Yes, here is a good place!

Then we build the fire and sound mantras for Agnihotra. On our minds is the knowledge that we are specifically working with the fire so that the energy of Ayers Rock will increase. So that the energy of all her eleven Ayers Rock brothers and sisters around the earth is increased. For the benefit of the world.

After our meditation, I tell Doreen that I feel our efforts are good, but I am a bit surprised the Aborigines have not connected with us. I have told them we are here to help this place and to help the earth. Why have they not responded?

After breakfast, Doreen and I return to Ayers Rock with climbers who, when we arrive, begin climbing this sacred place. Again, Doreen and I are not interested. We believe climbing is a sacrilege here.

As the climbing begins, we sit with our backs touching the red skin of this sacred place, and Doreen begins writing. After a time, and after much pondering about 'the right and wrong' of what I am thinking to do, I decide to walk up a short pathway that goes to a cave. It only takes me a moment or two to reach the narrow cave and enter.

Inside the cave, about five feet back from the entrance, I sit quietly looking out at the vast green area that is green because of all the rain. I feel like a cave man of old times. Then I correct myself that I feel like an Aborigine.

At that moment, THEY ALL ENTER MY CONSCIOUSNESS. Aborigine spirits, many of them!

I begin saying over and over to them, "We have come to help. We have come to help. We have come to help." Over and over I say this and they are listening, but they are not grasping the significance.

They are not unfriendly and they do not tell me to leave. Yet, they are not understanding.

I keep telling them over and over that I am not here to bother them. I am not intruding. But I see they are not understanding, and so I leave the cave.

I climb down to Doreen and tell her I am unhappy because they do not understand.

When the ranger bus driver decides it is time to go to Maggie Springs, he tells us this is the sacred water hole for the Aborigines. They used it only for drinking and never for washing. Then, the White Men came down from the North with animals and they, both the men and animals, drank the sacred water. Plus, both the men and animals bathed and washed in the sacred water.

This was a great violation, and the Aborigines moved away from this sacred spring and have never drunk the water again.

Doreen and I understand the need to right this wrong. We go to Maggie Springs and put into the water a healing crystal plus healing Agnihotra ash coming from this morning's sacred fire.

We realize the Aborigine spirits may understand what we are doing at Maggie Springs, but they do not understand everything. They know that the plunk of the sacred healing crystal hitting the water has broken the karma of the violation. They are understanding that but there is more they do not understand.

Later, in meditation, I try desperately to make myself understood by the Aborigine spirits, and I am saying that Ayers Rock is important for all the planet. When I say I am working with the SUN OF THE FULL MOON, they understand!

I tell them I am an Earth Mother and Doreen is an Earth Mother and we are working with Ayers Rock, this magnetic center, to help Mother Earth.

CRACK!!!!

With my psychic inner ears, I hear this.

THEY UNDERSTAND!!!!

They understand exactly what I am saying, and in that instant, I hear their sticks beating communication throughout the Aborigine spirit world. A communication telling everyone we are here!

I know we are fully, completely accepted. Never mind if they do not understand exactly our work, but they trust us.

Later, at the resort complex where we are staying, I wander into a shop and buy two Aborigine sticks labeled in the shop as 'musical instruments'. When I show them to Doreen, she says they are the same type used to send the messages.

Now we are putting our concentration on going to the Olgas, sibling of Ayers Rock. When we arrive, we climb a short distance to an ancient rock cluster called Lookout Point. We are told this is on a straight line to Ayers Rock.

My body feels a VERY STRONG ley line running between the two, and I am understanding that Ayers Rock uses this ley line to stimulate the Olgas.

We place Agnihotra ash here.

At my feet are bright rocks containing copper, iron, etc. The Olgas, which I think lived millions of years at the bottom of water, is a mineral gold mine.

A fan-shaped lizard, very small, makes his appearance, and the ranger who has brought Doreen and me here, says there are also huge lizards. Some as long as two meters.

Yes, the Olgas are fascinating.

And yes, my memory returns to fascination as I am writing this to you.

But, especially I wanted to tell you about our use of Agnihotra during our Ayers Rock/Olgas visit. Agnihotra is a cleanser and I feel very strongly that it should be useful today, 2018, to cleanse the world, especially Japan that has high radiation.

GLOSSARY

CHAPTER 1: SUNSHINE COAST, AUSTRALIA

Vortexes and Symbols: http://www.starelders.net
https://www.starknowledge.org

THE SYMBOLS, The Universal Symbols and Laws of Creation: A Divine Plan by Which One Can Live. The Heavenly Hosts, The Servants of Creator. © 1996 by Standing Elk. One Eye Productions.

THE VORTEXES, The Universal Symbols and Laws of Creation. (The 11:11 MorningStar Vortexes Book) ©1997 by Standing Elk. One Eye Productions.

Glass House Mountains:
Ancient Geology. The Glass House Mountains tell a story. http://www.mary-cairncross.com.au/glasshouse-mountains-geology.php

----

CHAPTER 2: FIRST DAYS IN AUSTRALIA

Map of Uluru and Kata Tjuta: http://uluruhoponhopoff.com.au/timetable/

CHAPTER 3: AYERS ROCK (ULURU), THE OLGAS (KATA TJUTA)

CLOSING THE ULURU CLIMB:
Why the closure of the Uluru climb is reason to celebrate.
https://www.ayersrockresort.com.au/blog/closing-the-uluru-climb

Tourism businesses – Voyages:
http://www.ilc.gov.au/Home/What-We-Do/Tourism-Businesses

Voyages Indigenous Tourism Australia:
https://www.voyages.com.au

CHAPTER 4: ALICE SPRINGS AND CORROBOREE ROCK

Alice Springs Expeditions, John Stafford:
https://www.alicespringsexpeditions.com.au

Alice Springs Visitor Information Center:
https://www.discovercentralaustralia.com/contact-us/alice-springs-visitor-information-centre

----

CHAPTER 5: JAPAN JOURNEY BEGINS

Healing by Contacting Your Cells:
https://www.authorhouse.com/bookstore/bookdetail.aspx?bookid=SKU-000412314

Video: 10,000 Japanese singing Beethoven's Ode to Joy:
https://www.youtube.com/watch?v=X6s6YKlTpfw&frags=pl%2Cwn

Scientific Aspects of Agnihotra; Agnihotra and Radioactivity:
https://www.agnihotra.org/2018/02/16/scientific-aspects-of-agnihotra-agnihotra-and-radioactivity-2/

CHAPTER 6: OUR TALKS IN SHIBUYA (TOKYO)

Video: Agnihotra Demonstration:
https://www.youtube.com/watch?v=uRnsOD2zPO8

Scientific Aspects of Agnihotra; Agnihotra and Radioactivity:
https://www.agnihotra.org/2018/02/16/scientific-aspects-of-agnihotra-agnihotra-and-radioactivity-2/

CHAPTER 8: SYMPHONY OF PEACE PRAYRS, MOUNT FUJI

Symphony of Peace Prayers:
http://www.symphonyofpeaceprayers.com/soppatfuji/sopp-2018/

The Fuji Declaration:
https://fujideclaration.org

Mount Fuji: https://volcanocafe.wordpress.com/2014/05/21/mount-fuji-fujisan/

Tectonic Plates diagram, Mount Fuji:
https://volcanocafe.files.wordpress.com/2014/05/fig-4-philippine_sea_plate_br-2.jpg

----

CHAPTER 10: AUSTRALIA 1989 VISIT
Video: Agnihotra Demonstration:
https://www.youtube.com/watch?v=uRnsOD2zPO8

VORTEX SYMBOLS

Chief Golden Light Eagle and Grandmother SilverStar have given us valuable information on how to use powerful energy fields to help Mother Earth and all that live on her. This information has come from sacred ceremony and the information is available through these books:

THE SYMBOLS, The Universal Symbols and Laws of Creation: A Divine Plan by Which One Can Live. The Heavenly Hosts, The Servants of Creator. © 1996 by Standing Elk. One Eye Productions.

THE VORTEXES, The Universal Symbols and Laws of Creation. (The 11:11 MorningStar Vortexes Book) ©1997 by Standing Elk. One Eye Productions.

http://www.starelders.net
https://www.starknowledge.org

One Vortex equals two combined Star Law Symbols.

The **Vortex of Light, Sound and Vibration** is formed by joining the Symbol of the *Universal Law of Light, Sound and Vibration* with the Symbol of *Spiritual Law of Intuition*.

The **Vortex of Integrity** is formed by the *Universal Law of Free Will* combining with the *Spiritual Freedom of Man*. This is a free will planet and can only operate fully when there is complete spiritual freedom of man. There should be freedom with truth and honesty.

The **Vortex of Symmetry** is formed by combining the *Universal Law of Symmetry* with the *Spiritual Law of Equality*. Symmetry means balance between all things, both spiritual and material. As above, so below. Also, equality between male/female, left/right brain, etc.

The **Vortex of Strength, Health and Happiness** is formed with the combining of the *Universal Law of Movement and Balance* with the *Spiritual Strength, Health and Happiness*. In life one has to be balanced to move forward and also one has to move forward to be balanced. Balance is symmetry in motion. With movement and balance come strength and health and happiness.

The **Vortex of Right Relationship** is produced by combining the *Universal Law of Innocence, Truth and Family* with *Spiritual Protection of Family*. This is also a powerful Vortex of social relationship (based on truth) when the concept has moved from the individual to the group.

The **Vortex of Growth** is formed when the *Universal Law of Change* is combined with the *Spiritual Growth of Man*. Change is a basic tenant of life. With spiritual growth, all things thrive. All things change. Nothing is static. Therefore, both the individual and society need the spiritual growth of man. When humanity grows spiritually, then the Vortex of Growth flourishes. In the natural state, all things grow unhindered. With spiritual growth all things thrive.

The **Vortex of True Judgment** is formed by combining the *Universal Law of Judgment* with the *Spiritual Law of Karma*. All actions should be looked at through the eyes of the *Universal Law of Judgment* so that no harm is done and there is no karma. The latter, the consequences of action, can be turned into dharma, teaching. This law applies socially as well as environmentally.

The **Vortex of Perception** is formed by the combining of the *Universal Law of Perception* combined with the *Spiritual Law of Future Sight*. It is important to perceive the impact of one's actions and to use the gift of future sight. Needed now are planetary actions that affect in a good way the lives of the people in relationship to the air, the water, the land, the life on this planet.

The **Vortex of Connection to Life** is formed with the combining of the *Universal Law of Life* with the *Spiritual Law of Choice*. Life is enhanced by correct choices. It is diminished by poor choices. Therefore, choose wisely. Choice and Life are integrally connected.

The **Vortex of True Nature** is formed by the combining of the *Universal Law of Nature* with the *Spiritual Law of Protection*. Nature exists and thrives. It is up to mankind to protect Nature so that all life thrives on this planet.

The **Vortex of Love** is formed by combining the *Universal Law of Love* with the *Spiritual Law of Healing*. One has to have Love to give healing and to receive healing. Love is the greatest healer. People, Nature, all creatures, plants, cells, molecules, atoms, adamantine particles respond to Love. All have a consciousness. Love creates. Love heals. Love is the highest power of all.

A Vortex Ring is formed at the center of a circle of all Vortexes displayed together. This Vortex is called **Universal Unity and Spiritual Integrity**. All Vortexes bring unity. All Vortexes thrive with integrity. Integrity is the foundation of the Vortexes.

Printed in the United States
By Bookmasters